SALT OF PLEASURE

TWENTIETH-CENTURY FINNISH POETRY

Aili Jarvenpa

SALT OF PLEASURE: TWENTIETH-CENTURY FINNISH POETRY

Translated by Aili Jarvenpa

With an Introduction by
K. Börje Vähämäki

and

Photographs by Oliver and Robert Jarvenpa

A New Rivers Abroad Book

New Rivers Press 1983

Translations copyright © 1983 by Aili Jarvenpa
Library of Congress Catalog Card Number: 83-62081
ISBN: 0-89823-048-9
All rights reserved
Book Design: C. W. Truesdale
Keylining: Daren Sinsheimer
Typesetting: Peregrine Cold Type

Publication of *Salt of Pleasure* has been made possible by grants from the National Endowment for the Arts and the United Arts Council.

Salt of Pleasure has been manufactured in the United States of America for New Rivers Press, Inc. (C. W. Truesdale, editor/publisher), 1602 Selby Ave., St. Paul, MN 55104 in a first edition of 1500 copies.

In Memory of
FRANS MARPIO

SALT OF PLEASURE

Introduction, 9
Translator's Note, 21

Eino Leino, 25
Aaro Hellaakoski, 41
P. Mustapää, 45
Uuno Kailas, 53
Katri Vala, 61
Yrjö Jylhä, 69
Arvo Turtianinen, 75
Viljo Kajava, 87
Eeva-Liisa Manner, 95
Anja Vammelvuo, 105
Aila Meriluoto, 111
Helena Anhava, 119
Tuomas Anhava, 127
Eeva Kilpi, 133
Veijo Meri, 145
Pertti Nieminen, 153
Paavo Haavikko, 161
Mirkka Rekola, 167
Väinö Kirstinä, 173
Pentti Saarikoski, 181
Sirkka Turkka, 193
Pentti Saaritsa, 203
Hannu Mäkelä, 209
Tommy Tabermann, 215
Arto Melleri, 221
Jukka Vieno, 227

Acknowledgements, 223
Selected Bibliography, 236
Notes on Translator, Photographer,
    and Introducer, 238

INTRODUCTION

1. Background

To understand the traditions, attitudes and idiosyncrasies of the Finnish people, it is helpful to look at their geographical situation, for it is, to a great degree, the key to their political and cultural life. Situated between Scandinavian Sweden and Slavic Soviet Union, Finland's experiences have been intimately tied to those of her neighbors'. In fact, only upon declaring her independence in 1917 did Finland settle *between* the two countries. Previously, she had been, for some 650 years, a Swedish province and subsequently an autonomous Grand Duchy of the Russian Empire from 1809 to 1917.

The geography translates into a barren and fragile eco-system marked by great contrasts: dark-light, cold-warm, sea-land, lakes-forest, virgin land-urban centers, open bedrock-fertile former sea bottom. Even the political reality of Finland is tenuous. Finland is the only western democracy that stands along a more than 700-mile stretch face to face with the Soviet Union. Pentti Saarikoski expresses this in his poem, "Helsinki": "We sit here in the midst of our forests our backs to the giant."

The cultural picture comprises versatile elements. Besides the obvious cultural differences inherent in the bilingual status of the country (Finnish and Swedish are by constitution the national languages of Finland today), the longstanding, still perceptible division of the country into two cultural areas—a western and an eastern Finland—has been significant. These two cultural entities were a consequence of the settlement patterns. The Finns Proper and the Häme people who make up western Finland entered the Finnish mainland from the south and southeast, respectively, while eastern Finland was settled from the West by the Savo people and the Karelians. The indigenous dissimilarities were, however, further accentuated and given permanence by the fact that western Finland was drawn into cultural influences of Swedish Uppland, i.e. the Stockholm area, while eastern Finland was subsumed under the cultural dominance first of Novgorod, later St. Petersburg. It is no coincidence that the first boundary between Sweden and Russia, defined in 1323, coincides with the line that culturally divides west and east Finland, nor that the dialectologists delineate the major Finnish dialects along the same geographical line. Not only are the impulses Scandinavian vs. Slavic, they are also Catholic, later Lutheran vs. Greek Orthodox. The Swedish segment of the population, it is important to recognize, still lives today within the western Finnish area.

Having noted a set of built-in contrasts, I will proceed to show that Finland today is an uncommonly homogeneous society and, furthermore, that this homogeneity can be explained with reference not only to the historical experiences of the nation but also to the age old incompatibilities.

An eastern province of Sweden for centuries, Finland had a population whose majority language, Finnish, enjoyed little or no recognition except as a church language, and whose principal source of livelihood was farming, hunting and fishing, modes of economy that do not command organized social structure. In 1809 Finland found herself in a precarious situation. The educated class, the administrators, the intelligentsia spoke Swedish, yet less than twenty percent were Swedish. The constitution, the legal system, the social and political institutions (all of which Finland, as a Grand Duchy, was allowed to preserve) were Swedish. Thus, when the source that had fed societal life in Finland was abruptly cut off, the scene was set for an identity crisis.

The Swedish leadership, whose Finnishness was not in doubt, had to adapt gradually to an inevitable eclipse as the Finnish majority realized their status. The only viable alternative for the new autonomous entity was to shift to Finnish language and identity. The crux of the matter, however, was the question: what does it mean to be Finnish?

The void was soon filled in almost fairy tale fashion. Lönnrot, Runeberg and Snellman, who were freshmen roommates at Turku University in 1822, were to respond in three dimensions. In a true Herderian national romantic tradition, Elias Lönnrot gave the Finns a legendary history, a national spirit, a national soul. The *Kalevala* and the *Kanteletar* (an epic compiled by Lönnrot from epic narrative folk poetry collected in Karelia, and its lyrical counterpart) served, respectively, as Herder's philosophy maintained, the purpose of discovering genuinely Finnish cultural traditions: a mythology, a value system, cultural institutions. The influence of the Kalevalaic poetry on Finnish culture in general and Finnish literature in particular is too overwhelming to describe. It has entered the life of the people. It has become inseparably ingrained in the Finnish way of thought.

Johan Ludvig Runeberg, in a classisist, humanistic tradition, wrote national romantic poetry in Swedish that generated *pride in being Finnish*. His idealistic, patriotic *Tales of Ensign Stol*, which includes the Finnish national anthem, "Our Land," formulated the mythology of the recent past, raising the Finnish soldier of the war of 1808-09 and his humble heroism to legendary heights. Furthermore, Runeberg's admiration for the simple, unrelenting and god-fearing common Finnish man added to the democratic foundation of the Finnish cause.

Johan Vilhelm Snellman was a philosopher, a journalist, a senator. In his Hegelian concepts of the national state, Snellman provided the ultimate answer. In order that a Finnish national state could emerge, he felt that the political and cultural institutions must be founded on one language, Finnish. The two major vehicles to achieve this goal were (1) education in the Finnish language generally for the masses and in the form of higher education for the future national leaders, and (2) literature. The special emphasis on literature is significant. Snellman believed in the dialectic process and saw literature as its principal tool.

10

The establishment of a national identity, of a sense of national pride, and a clear national program in preparing for eventual nationhood were the three dimensions in which 19th century Finland proceeded, but not without turmoil. The cultural identity emerged in a happy compromise between western Finland, the tradition of the establishment, and eastern Finland, the source of the Kalevalaic folk culture. The standardization of written Finland, which compromised western as well as eastern dialectical traits and in which Lönnrot's mediating stance became decisive, represents this new unification of cultural traditions. The shift from Swedish to Finnish in various facets of Finnish institutional life did not proceed without controversy; the nature of such a transition presupposes opposition. The Finnish side needed an adversary, a measure with which to record the progress; the Swedish side would not yield its privileges voluntarily. Nevertheless, the educational program was successful: Finland moved from virtually total illiteracy among the Finns at the beginning of the 19th century to near full literacy by 1900.

Young Finland was democratic in attitude. Since no Finnish language court tradition had existed, the transition to the status of a civilized people was allowed, even prescribed, to occur in a broad, sweeping movement. However, a Finnish speaking upper class inevitably evolved, the democratic ideals notwithstanding. Industrialization and urbanization led to the birth of new social classes, a working class and a class of landless tenant farmers. The unrestrained capitalism of early industrial Europe produced inequalities and social injustices. While poverty had largely been due to natural conditions in the older economies, the injustices and inequalities of the latter half of the 1800's and 1900's were felt to be man made. Except for the so-called oppression years, the years of russification efforts emanating from the Czar at the turn of the century, attention focused on pressing social issues. The labor movement tested its power with a general strike in 1905. Finland got a democratic constitution with universal suffrage in 1906, which, however, could not secure democratic processes and democratic implementations since the Parliament was rendered impotent by unilateral imperial decrees from the Czar. The rifts in Finnish society were deep enough to lead to the Civil War of Finland in 1918, only months after Finland declared herself independent from the revolution-ridden Soviet Union, and for reasons and ambitions similar to those of the socialist revolution in Russia.

Despite the deep wounds left by the Civil War, wounds that have only slowly healed and with some scars still showing today, I would claim, not that it united the people, but that it harshly opened the eyes of the Finnish people to the realities of Finland: it was a modern, democratic, industrial state where the regional stratification was no longer relevant but where the social strata were the new reality. The legislative activity of the 'twenties was intense and progressive. The move to the right in the 'thirties reflected the fascistic inclinations in Europe in general and in Germany in particular, under whose cultural and political influence Finland was under World

11

War II. The two wars against the Soviet Union, the Winter War of 1939-40 and the Continuation War of 1941-44, left the Finns with a major insight: "geo-politically our position is unchangeable, outside our control, but culturally and socially we are our own masters." One of the characters in Väinö Linna's war novel, *The Unknown Soldier*, says, "The Soviet Union won, but Finland was a good second."

The building of a welfare state that treasures the cultural traditions, that is committed to democracy in deed and attitude, and that is founded on the ideal that income gaps should be minimal has made Finland what it is today, a post-industrial nation with a stable political scene and homogeneous ideals.

2. The Traditions

The *Kalevala*, called the national epic of Finland, and the *Kanteletar*, its lyrical counterpart, were both compiled and published by Elias Lönnrot and today occupy a position in Finnish consciousness similar to that of the *Bible*. They are revered for their magnanimity, for their larger than life spirit, and for their universal symbolism, yet they are not necessarily read much. The *Kalevala* has served as the ultimate court of appeal, the standard of verification, as a guide to the true concepts of right and wrong, of good and evil, in short as a world view and philosophy of life. What we can read in Eino Leino in explicit Kalevala meter and imagery we find between the lines in other Finnish poets.

While many 19th century poets, often futilely, struggled to fit the Finnish language—a non-Indoeuropean tongue whose *belles lettres* tradition is but 120 years old—into foreign, mostly classical molds, the indigenous poetry had an established meter. The Kalevala meter splendidly allows the prosodic characteristics of Finnish, particularly the stress and quantity oppositions, not only to prevail but to blossom. Yet, stylistically, Finnish folk poetry has been of only indirect significance. Despite Eino Leino's literary Kalevalaic poetry, P. Mustapää's deceptively simple, folk song inspired poems and some of Arvo Turtiainen's and Paavo Haavikko's works, the greater impact of Kalevalaic poetry derives from the poetic attitude and value systems inherent in the folk poetry, and the confidence in the intrinsic creativity, in the poetic powers of the Finnish language that emanated from the *Kalevala*.

In order to comprehend the incomparable influence that the *Kalevala* has exerted on subsequent poetry in Finland, it is important to recognize that the Finns view their epic as a timeless epitome of the national consciousness. There is a symbiotic union between the epic world and the various poetic worlds of all of Finland's major poets. The elements that I feel are clearly running through from folk poetry through the entire poetic tradition of the Finns include: (1) a mythology of their own; (2) a monistic, pantheistic union of man and nature; (3) a democratic, non-individualisic outlook; (4) a reflective melancholy; and (5) something I will call proud humility.

The mythology, Finno-Ugric in origin, offers a rich body of national, original symbols. Äijö in Leino's "Äijö's Song," the opening poem of this collection, is the Finnish creator who will exclude man from his new creation because people have become a pack of hyenas, but who will invite the mythological

> powers of the land, rulers of the water
> all of my eternal brothers,
> I will invite *Kimmo*, the spirit of the hearth,
> *Kammo* from death's entrance hall.

A mythological presence is also felt in some essential shamanistic imagery that involves, as did the shamanistic religion of the ancient Finns, transcendental travel in the shape of a bird, e.g. to the land of the dead. This is exemplified in Aaro Hellaakoski's "Moonlight in the Forest." Other mythological elements found in several poems in this volume that are irrevocably rooted in Finnish mythology include the sun theft motif, the bear cult, the elk symbolism, various spirits and deities, the rowan tree, the sea and the birches.

The union of man and nature and the monism of the *Kalevala* breathes on almost every page of this anthology. These are particularly revealed in Eeva-Liisa Manner's poetry in which she imaginatively merges with the forest, Viljo Kajava's short poems, and Eeva Kilpi's biological inclinations and receptiveness to the voice of nature. They place man in tune with nature as well as apply a perspective that yields "correct" proportions, as illustrated in Arto Melleri's poem, "Proportions."

The democratic attitude that pervades Finnish literature as a whole derives from two sources, from the Kalevala world and from the very conditions under which the literary tradition in Finland emerged in the mid-1800's. There was no Finnish nobility, the authors came from the populace, wrote about ordinary, often backwoods, characters, and perceived their audience as the Finnish people, not an exclusive elite. The democratic concept is quite compatible with the concept of man as a creature of nature. It encompasses a non-belligerant, non-individualistic philosophy and a respect for the less fortunate. Analytical intellectualism is often perceived by Finnish poets as fundamentally undemocratic, as exclusive, and as a form of execution of power, and thus something to reject, or at least avoid. Kilpi, Turtiainen, P. Mustapää, Saaritsa and Tabermann concern themselves with such questions.

The reflective melancholy that characterizes Finnish poetry may represent Slavic influence. It is, however, a predominant trait of Finnish folk poetry and folk songs. Thus Finnish folk songs are typically in a minor key. The lament-poetry tradition is still alive in Karelia, and the great characters of the *Kalevala*, Väinämöinen, Ilmarinen and Lemminkäinen, never hesitate to give voice to their grief, weeping openly and humbly in song. Thus, when Leino's Äijö

> sang a song throughout the night
> from the deepest reaches of his soul

13

he did so in the truest Kalevala tradition, including the hyperbolically expressed depth of his feeling. When Pertti Nieminen, Eeva Kilpi, Helena Anhava and Väinö Kirstinä emphasize the simple values in life, their reflections resemble Kalavalaic basics; the melancholy is subdued, yet present.

The last tradition in Finnish poetry singled out here, proud humility, is difficult to define. The *Kalevala*, and more explicitly J.L. Runeberg in the Finnish national anthem, reiterates the premise that "Finland is poor, shall so remain." The poverty has fostered a philosophy marked by asceticism, self-sacrifice and humility. Still, that same poverty is a cource of pride except, of course, in Leino's Nietszchean poem, "I." Incidentally, this ingrained notion of economic inferiority has in fact, until quite recently, been a major obstacle for Finnish businessmen in marketing their products internationally. Most Finnish public speakers refer apologetically to Finland as small and poor, while, at the same time, portraying this "fact" as the country's greatest virtue. I feel that many poems in this volume reflect a pride and a humility that give them a unique tone and flavor.

3. The Poets and the Poetry

The 20th century was born at the peak of a literary period in Finland named National Neo-Romanticism by its foremost representative, Eino Leino. Recent scholarship labels the period National Symbolism. It began as a counter-movement to the socially concerned, prosaic realism of the 1880's and early 1890's and is the literary counterpart to the broad cross-disciplinary Karelia-enthusiasm that emerged at the end of the 19th century, appropriately called Karelianism.

National Neo-Romanticism can best be understood as a phenomenon with multiple causes. Sociopolitically the russification efforts, the so-called Russian oppression that intensified at the turn of the century, caused the intelligentsia to transfer its interest from social issues to the larger and more pressing problem: preserving the national identity, the national existence. The rising working class, intensely ideological, was a socially relevant factor. Furthermore, the symbolist spirit in Europe, particularly French and Danish symbolism and Nietszcheanism of Germany, reached opportune soil in Finland. Eino Leino, in his poetry, scholarly writing and cultural journalism, epitomizes these components. His *Whit Songs* and other Kalevala-inspired poetry created new national symbols in the Karelianistic spirit. His Nietszchean bent shows itself in certain poems, e.g. the poem "I." Leino was a national cosmopolitan, a non-conformist Bohemian without chauvinism, but with a Finnish heart.

Leino alone in this volume represents the first two decades of this century. Finland-Swedish poetry, which is not included because of space limitations and other practical concerns, experienced an early lyrical modernism led by Edith Södergran and Elmer Diktonius, who both published their first poetry in 1916. Finland-Swedish modernism did not find

14

immediate response nor counterpart in the Finnish language poetry of Finland. Closest to it came the Torch Bearers, an informal group of young poets who adopted the name of a calendar that had appeared in 1924. In 1928 they began to publish a journal of the same name. In a society still suffering open wounds from the Civil War of 1918, this new generation that looked forward rather than back, with neither guilt nor shame, was refreshing. Its very manifesto breathes the new attitude:

> Life is sacred. We love it.

> Art is sacred. We serve it.

> No program prevails for more than a generation and no truth is eternal. The purpose of life is the continuation of life.

> Therefore we have only one objective: spiritual freedom, the freedom to criticize and deal with everything. We do not recognize authorities, because their position makes them cowards before life.

> See: how marvelously young our country is, how full of strength!

> Come, do not fear: you have been chosen to create something new and great.

> Break the link that squeezes our hearts: be yourselves, acknowledge life.

This program was open enough to allow any individual idiosyncrasies as long as optimism and a sense of limitless potential was shared by all members of the group. The other dimension in the Torch Bearers' credo was the internationalism reflected in their slogan: "Open the windows to Europe." Through those windows entered German expressionism, exoticism, and a genuine interest in the now established Finland-Swedish modernism and its free verse. The tone is, however, predominantly emotional, and the life line thus short. The significance of the Torch Bearers is less in the artistic arena and more in its inspirational, youthful radicalism that allowed its former members—quietly dispanded during the 1930's—to pursue their individual careers. The Torch Bearers were instrumental in the emergence of a subsequent group, the Kiila (The Wedge), which took, as their program, leftist, radical social criticism.

The most typical Torch Bearer was Katri Vala. Ecstasy and visual and sensory images characterize her poems. Her obsession with light particularly witnesses to her sensory ecstasy. Her tragic fate (she died of tuberculosis at 43) brings forth imagery in reverse. She is equally ecstatic and intense in her tragic experience. Her few years of marriage and motherhood gave a social dimension to her later poetry, and a certain softness which yet remained uncompromising.

The other Torch Bearers included in this collection, Uuno Kailas, Yrjö Jylhä and marginally Viljo Kajava, found their own individual styles and forms. Kailas epitomizes the role of Finnish poet during the period between the wars. His introverted personality, illness and poverty perhaps explain his ethical rigor, his relentless soul-serching and pursuit of purity.

15

Kailas shows influence of Baudelaire and later of German *Angst Dichtung* and confessional poetry. He combines ethical rigorism with esthetic stringency; his language is extremely disciplined, nearing laconic classicism.

Kailas' ethical rigor is, in fact, a prominent trait in Finnish 20th century poetry before World War II and is pronounced in Jylhä'spoetry as well. Kai Laitinen, author of a recent Finnish literary history, points out that the poets of the 'twenties and 'thirties, although not religious in terms of dogma and doctrine, still expound their ethical inquiries in religious terms, such as suffering, repentance, atonement and mercy. Kailas' tuberculosis and isolated existence gave his death poetry unforgettable power.

Death is also a major theme for Yrjö Jylhä. While Kailas was fragile and esoteric in appearance and attitude, Jylhä was masculine, virile and handsome. After Kailas' untimely death, Jylhä became the leading bearer of the rigorous ethical as well as esthetic tradition. His extensive translations of Shakespeare, Milton, LaFontaine, Heine the *Chanson de Roland* and English ballads, the high quality of which alone would give him a position in Finnish literary history, augmented his tendency toward rigid laconicism, exactitude in expression and masculine restraint. His last book, the collection *Kiirastuli (Purgatory*, 1941), is a war monument that deals with his personal experiences as an officer in the Winter War of 1939-40 and reflects Jylhä's true humanism in face of the reality of war. The power of these poems, some of which are my own favorites, lies in their simple, unembellished language and reflective tone.

The Torch Bearers appear to have been a group whose unifying elements were youthful enthusiasm and the non-ideological radicalism of the new generation of the 'twenties. While this group's significance lies in the esthetic attitude, the Killa emerged as a politically and socialistically oriented group of young poets of the 'thirties, represented in this volume by Arvo Turtiainen and Viljo Kajava. The Kiila must be seen as a leftist association deeply disturbed, on the one hand, by the rightist, blatantly fascist developments in Europe in the 'thirties and, on the other, by the persecution of Communists in Finland.

Labeling Turtiainen and Kajava as typical Kiila poets does not do justice to either one. In fact, while scholarship, by definition, is the assessment of allowable generalizations, this becomes difficult in characterizing these two poets for two reasons. Both authors have had productive careers that span four decades and, more importantly, poetry is always idiosyncratic. But their concern and identification with the proletariat of urban society, Helsinki and Tampere respectively, does bring a new dimension into Finnish poetry, and in that sense the Kiila exerted a more direct, yet less universal influence on Finnish poetry than did the Torch Bearers.

Turtiainen's ballads about Helsinki, about the Civil War, and about the working class bring to mind Master's *Spoon River Anthology*, which he translated into Finnish. "Shoemaker Nikke" is a powerful tribute to the simple man and is representative of his attitude.

16

Kajava is more overtly emotional, more radical in tone than Turtiainen. Both authors became love poets of note quite late in their careers. Kajava, due to international experiences and active translation work, broke with the Kiila in the late 1940's and became a modernist of the 'fifties and 'sixties. He is still productive today.

Two other poets with uncommonly lengthy poetic careers are Aaro Hellaakoski and P. Mustapää. Literary surveys often treat these poets together with the post-World War II literature as influential anticipators of the lyrical modernism of the 'fifties; yet Hellaakoski's debut occurred in 1916 and Mustapää's in the Torch Bearer's publications in the 'twenties.

Hellaakoski is an isolated early modernist in Finnish poetry. A natural scientist and teacher by profession, his interest in nature inevitably set him apart from the egocentricism, the isolation and ethical anguish that characterized the Torch Bearers. His heightened sense of self, his attitude toward nature and his desire for experimentation brought a moderistic vein into the Finnish poetry of the 'twenties that was not, however, adopted by others. The novel imagery of his poetry reflects his interest in painting and the fact that he had married into a family of sculptors. So it is not surprising that he makes strong connections with cubist painting and with futuristic poetry, particularly Apollinaire. After a period of silence (1928-1941) devoted to scholarly research, he resumed his poetic experimentation and paved the way for the modernism of the 'fifties.

P. Mustapää is the pseudonym of one of the most famous folklorists in Finland, Martti Haavio. He held the prestigious professorship in Finnish folklore at the University of Helsinki. Although he was affiliated with the Torch Bearers in his youth, Haavio, as Mustapää, was to become the master of the simple, non-intellectual (at least superficially) folk song tradition in Finnish poetry. He was not interested in the exoticism and in the inner conscience struggles of his contemporaries. Rather than demand or expect the impossible, he became a relativist with a sense of humor and an eye for proportions. As a poet Mustapää treasures wisdom; as a scholar Haavio respects intellectual analysis. Mustapää is very sparse in narrative, descriptive language. He draws few, deceptively simple pictures, and the undercurrents become powerful. A favorite theme of his, seen in two poems in this collection, is the concept of writing poems, or rather songs, "without words." This allows the inner architecture of the poem full realization, an interest that can also be seen in the work of Ezra Pound.

Kai Laitinen says about the immediate postwar literature in Finland that "The literature was written by grandfathers and grandsons; the generation of the fathers was nearly silent." The grandfathers, Turtiainen, Kajava, Hellaakoski and Mustapää, were joined by the granddaughters Anja Vammelvuo, Aila Meriluoto and Eeva-Liisa Manner. The war, perhaps perceived by women more markedly as insane, shattered all illusions of the young generation. As the 1920's became the decade of the young writers of Finland, so did the late 'forties and the 'fifties, and for very similar reasons.

The poem, "The Stone God," in Aila Meriluoto's collection *Lasimaalaus* (*Glass Painting*, 1946), became the catalyst of postwar sentiment. Published in a total of 25,000 copies, the volume verbalized the realization that the young generation was rising out of the ruins of the war "without faith, without mercy." While the pathos of this poem today may appear excessive, at the time it seemed both genuine and profound. This collection is considered in Finnish literature as the herald of European modernism, although formally still quite traditional.

The postwar poets moved definitively away from the uncompromising requirements of absolute, universal validity of the ethical questions. Similarly, beauty and truth were redefined. It is to be looked for and found in everyday life. The foreign influences of Ezra Pound, T.S. Eliot, Rainer Maria Rilke, etc., together with the shift towards relativism in ethics, a transformed conception of beauty, and the aggressive opposition mentality of Merilouto's, characterize the conditions into which the Finnish Modernism was born.

The term "Finnish Modernism" defies cohesive definition; there is no *Finnish* Modernism as distinct from the international trends in the poetries of the 'fifties, and Modernism is not a finite program. We, therefore, have to settle for some detectable phenomena. The first is the language. Meter and other elements of *written* poetry are abolished. *Speech* becomes the criterion. Haavikko explicitly says that he avoids putting anything down on paper. He would rather run the risk of forgetting or losing an idea or formulation than write it down, because as soon as it is noted on paper it is subject to the rhetoric of written language. Turtiainen's frequent use of urban slang, Saarikoski's employment of political and commercial jargon further expand the range of linguistic expression available to the poet. Paavo Haavikko, the leading modernist poet in the 'fifties and 'sixties, consciously exploits language based on the realization that language creates reality, illustrated in his poem, "When I Now Tell You About the Emperor." Haavikko's poetic mind, however, goes far beyond metapoetry and metalanguage. In an interview about the role and responsibility of the poet, Haavikko states that he finds the power of language quite frightening unless the poet reckons with his or her ultimate problem: how to take the treacherous symbols of language and shape them into the truth. This is, in fact, the central thrust of the modernist poet: to transcend the conventions of the semantics of language and capture the real truth. The traditional value systems, the traditional compartmentalization of reality, the traditional modes of expression and conceptualization were no longer adequate. Truth is comples, reality is not static. Many Modernists adopt a comprehensive historical attitude. Paavo Haavikko is fascinated by the conflict between individual and institution, between the historical and the present. The individual is always part of some institution, lives several roles simultaneously that are entirely inseparable and thus apparently contradictory. In 1958 Haavikko wrote:

Where does the voice in us come from? What is in the eyes?
Speech flows in the fleeting world
Speech flows in the fleeting world
and you must yourself know almost everything.

The imagery of the Modernist, often capricious, sometimes inaccessible, but always to be given the benefit of the doubt, emerges out of hatred for the falsity always inherent in well defined, confined value systems as well as of the need to redefine reality completely. Thomas Anhava's poem, "The Sky Has Wings," expresses this realization:

I remember everything. Everything happens.
Everything at once,
and gloriously at once like the autumn sun,
October brightness, or the sea's deep warmth.

While Haavikko explores the institutional historical dimension,; Eeva-Liisa Manner, whose collection *Tämä matka* (*This Journey*, 1956) represents a modernist manifesto, and P. Mustapää develop the mythological dimension combining old and new myths. The two poets also share an interest in music. Mustapää's lyrical inspiration is the simple folk song, Manner's the complex world of orchestral music.

Tuomas Anhava is the theoretician of Modernism in Finland. He introduced new criticism into Finland in his essays as well as in his translations of Ezra Pound and T.S. Eliot. Thus he kept a sensitive finger on the pulse of Modernism in the larger perspective. Manner, Haavikko and Anhava bring a theoretical awareness, an intellectual exactitude, into what is essentially an untheoretical, and hence creative and alive Finnish literature.

The 'sixties are known as the decade of politically engaged poetry. The premise was that the complexity of reality must include the political reality and ideological conflicts as well. Pentti Saarikoski became the leading leftist social critic, incorporating in his language political slogans and proletarian expressions. His political engagement soon lessened as his talent lay not in politics but in poetry. The 'sixties, internationally an era of political unrest and turbulence, of student revolts, etc., have left little of lasting quality in the domain of ideological poetry. In fact, several poems from the 'seventies included here comment on the shortcomings of overtly political poetry; Kirstinä's "Propaganda Art" emphasizes the volatile life of propagandistic art, Helena Anhava dares the young generation not to "use trite ready-made phrases." The misgivings about the "engaged poetry" were founded on its essentially ahistorical attitude and the danger of offering answers rather than questions.

The Modernist tradition was, at the same time, taken further by Mirkka Rekola, who emerged as a master of poetic expression in the 'sixties. Her poetry is extremely difficult to translate because of the complexity she, like Haavikko, vests in seemingly simple poems. Other new poets of the decade were Kirstinä, Nieminen and Saaritsa. Kirstinä's social criticism is radical, but humanistic rather than political. Saaritsa, also

19

considered a leftist poet, has his orientation in the universal and international—he has translated Latin American radical poetry. Nieminen, a specialist on and translator of Chinese poetry, opened channels to oriental thinking. Thus, at the advent of the 'seventies, the Finnish poetic scene was expanded in all directions, political, geographical, philosophical and historical.

The reaction to the expansionism of the 'sixties is a clear shift to short reflective poetry that is quiet, inconspicuous, and unpretentious, but honest. The new tone is provided by authors who had established careers as prose writers: Eeva Kilpi, Helena Anhava and Veijo Meri.

The short poetry of everyday life, the renewed interest in nature poetry and the like, has been seen as escapism, as a sign of growing tired of being the conscience of the world. It is, however, more likely that it reflects the new reality of a world that has become ever smaller. Regional and national entities have lost their significance. There is, on the other hand, only the individual who, in Haavikko's words, "must know almost everything," and, on the other, the world at large that, furthermore, faces the threat of destruction. Nature poetry carries overtones of fears of pollution and distorted balance. Love, death, suffering, joy can be experienced by the individual alone, but the individual is also a member of the human race; hence the universality of the individual's moments, fate. In Eeva Kilpi's love and death poetry, so quiet and simple, the naked, sensitive and giving human soul speaks with tremendous power. Helena Anhava and Sirkka Turkka, although different from Kilpi in temperament and personality, write prose-influenced short poems of lasting impact. The strong female voice in Finnish poetry is in line with the democratic tradition in Finland; it is versatile and quite audible in this collection as well as in Finnish poetry at large.

The reflective poem is also Hannu Mäkelä's trademark. Known also as a writer of children's books, Mäkelä possesses a sensitivity and a mobile imagination that give his poetry a soft, dreamy quality. The three youngest poets in this volume, Tommy Tabermann, Arto Melleri, and Jukka Vieno, symptomatically reflect a concern for Finnish traditions, even Finnish mythology. The identity quest of today's rootless citizen of the world takes him to the family, the very roots that feed him: Jukka Vieno's "land of the white lily" is where home is.

K. Börje Vähämäki
University of Minnesota

20

TRANSLATOR'S NOTE

In the past, the work of leading poets of smaller countries, especially those with minor languages such as Finland, was rarely accessible to the rest of the world. Fortunately this situation has begun to improve in recent years. It is important that outstanding poetry of all countries is made available in translation in order to promote an awareness and sensitivity that we are all of one world. Richard Jones and Kate Daniels, Editors of the literary journal *Poetry East*, state in the Fall 1981 issue, "For American readers, Finnish writing represents a window through which can be seen freshly the dichotomy and paradox of the individual and society."

This collection contains the work of 26 Finnish poets in English translation. The poems have been selected as representative of the best in Twentieth Century Finnish poetry. I am grateful to the many persons without whose help and encouragement this book could not have been possible. I especially wish to thank K. Börje Vähämäki, Associate Professor of Finnish, Department of Scandinavian, University of Minnesota. He has written the Introduction and has been a special consultant throughout the many phases of this project. His expert counsel and assistance have been invaluable.

I am deeply indebted to Michael Dennis Browne, nationally known poet and Professor of English, University of Minnesota, who instructed me a few years ago in a special directed study course in translating. He has continued to be very supportive. I thank Emilie Buchwald, editor of the poetry journal *Milkweed Chronicle*, who published my first poetry translations (several poems by Eeva Kilpi) in the Spring/Summer 1981 issue. Those poems are included in this collection, sometimes in somewhat different form.

I also wish to thank the following individuals who have encouraged me and for whom I have done translations: Dr. Michael Karni, Editor of *Finnish Americana*, a journal of Finnish American history and culture, New Brighton, Minnesota; Dr. Robert Matson, 1st Vice President and Editor-in-Chief of the Finnish American Literary Heritage Foundation, Portland, Oregon; and Dr. Michael Loukinen, Associate Professor of Sociology, Northern Michigan University, Marquette, Michigan, who is also producer and director of the award-winning documentary film, *Finnish American Lives*, and his latest film, *Tradition Bearers*. I also want to thank Timo Poropudas, Editor of *Työmies-Eteenpäin*, for his generous assistance and encouragement and Kalevi Sissonen, Editor of *Aikamme*, who has been very supportive.

I am deeply grateful to Roberta Malraison, poet and editor of small press magazines, who has been especially supportive in numerous ways, and Sue Ann Martinson, poet and editor of *Sing Heavenly Muse!*, for her

21

special assistance.

I would particularly like to extend my gratitude to Inkeri Väänänen-Jensen, Finnish-American translator of Finnish short stories, who has generously advised me and provided me with resource materials. I also want to thank Tuulikki Sinks, instructor of Finnish at the University of Minnesota and the International Institute, for her encouragement and support.

I express special appreciation to C.W. Truesdale, Editor/Publisher of New Rivers Press. He actively took the initiative in making this project possible, continuing his commitment of publishing translations of less accessible languages, such as his previously published collections of Hungarian and Catalan poetry. A poet of note, he has been a major consultant on the final versions of poetry in this collection. The work has progressed smoothly and efficiently, making the entire project rewarding and stimulating.

Finally and foremost, I thank my family, my children, for their love and assistance. I especially thank my husband, whose encouragement and support is constant and daily.

I wish I that I could have taken a copy of this book to Jyväskylä, Finland, and personally presented it to my cousin, Frans Marpio, who died in September 1982 at the age of 84, and in whose memory I dedicate this work. Sweet, gentle man, Frans would have understood. Perpetual scholar with a world vision, he shared his enthusiasm with me. For Christmas 1978, he sent me a book of Eeva Kilpi's poems (*Runoja 1972-1976*) and thus planted a seed from which this book evolved.

—Aili Jarvenpa

SALT OF PLEASURE

EINO LEINO

EINO LEINO
(1878-1926)

Eino Leino was the first major Finnish poet. He was the center of Finnish cultural life and a strong influence on other leading artists, including composer Jean Sibelius and painter Akseli-Gallen-Kallela. He gave direction to Finnish poetry in many different areas, adopting that role consciously. Leino was also a prolific writer of plays, novels, essays and newspaper columns. A skilled translator, he introduced Finns to Dante and to the French and German classical theater. Like Yeats, with whom he has been compared, Leino was inspired by symbolism and a strong national folk tradition.

A number of lyric poems, especially his masterwork, the first volume of *Helkavirsiä* (Whit Songs I, 1903), comprise Leino's most mature period, 1902-1908. He chose the themes of his *Whit Songs* from foreign as well as Finnish myths, legends, fairytales and ballads and imbued them with his own religious, psychological and philosophical ideas. The connections between Leino's *Whit Songs* and the Finnish epic poem, *Kalevala*, are strong. Leino's Nietzschean bent is sometimes revealed, as in the poems "Ylermi" and "Mina" (I). *Whit Songs I* was translated into English by Keith Bosley in 1978.

Helkavirsiä II (Whit Songs, 1916) is also considered among Leino's best works. In it he reveals how World War I crushed the optimism of the previous century. His message is prophetic and apocalyptic.

The intellectual background and the symbolism of Leino's poetry continue to have a strong impact. Yet he remains a mystery. Leino was full of contradictions, striving ceaselessly to create and renew himself and to influence those around him.

26

ÄIJÖ'S SONG

He was Äijö, born alone,
began alone, died alone,
sat on the edge of a cloud,
watched the world go by,
sang a song throughout the night
from the deepest reaches of his soul,
and concealed nothing
from the coming generation:

"I once believed in man,
I no longer believe,
people are a pack of hyenas,
evil, envious, shackled,
if someone should rise above them,
him they stab forever,
rejoicing within their breasts:
he is no better than we!

"I once believed in man,
I no longer weep, don't rejoice,
their joys will pass,
their misfortunes too,
I know my own cynicism,
I do not grieve about it, nor regret,
it's the victory of many struggles,
my payment for a thousand losses.

"Once I created man
in my own image,
they took on my faults,
abused my sensitivity,
I want to create a new species,
quiet, with reserved strength,
to travel the land, cross the sea
as with a sufferer's smile.

"Perhaps I'm now too old,
have become a child again,
I cannot stand my past,
even though I understand it;
I sang a song reflecting the moment,
I sang of pleasure, created pictures,
fantasized my desires:
all of that is gone from me.

"It has fled, will never return,
the faith of new peoples,
hope of truth's victory,
the love of the infinite,
people are a pack of hyenas,
that I created, that I will destroy,
I will bring forth a new creation,
a new one for my own joy.

"I will exclude man altogether,
invite as guests
powers of the land, rulers of the water,
all of my eternal brothers,
I will invite Kimmo, the spirit of the hearth,
Kammo, from death's entrance hall,
imprisoned forces I will free,
I will begin a new age."

I

1.

I was in the beginning

I
grew up near the Almighty
and all of it was I.

I am the world's thought,
work's yield of a thousand strong,
beginning, also end of life.

Others are variations:
the collective mind
is the highest.

2.

The self is the sweetest might,
that which is your birthright:
never give it away!

They are wrong, those who
speak thus of self-sacrifice:
good deeds elevate you,
bad deeds lower you.

An individual's legacy is sacred.

Guard carefully that precious gift
or if you waste it, disappear
like a star from the sky:
die as a fire of emptiness!

3.

Everything is in you: time
eternity, life, nature,
fatherland and humanity,
a seed of the greatest, the meanest.
What you are is up to you,
remember the extent of your will,
the road is prepared, the distance set,
the mountain to climb: freedom.

Travel toward the highest
crest of your happiness,
fulfill what you know, what you want,
and you fulfill God's will,
as you ascend, you lift the cover of the sky,
as you descend, you stifle life,
you become your own burden,
a cloud covering the sun from others.

As you travel, hold worlds in your arms,
step throughout the spectrum of time,
put on a shirt of battle
made from the steel of your deepest wish,
from the silver of dreams,
from the copper of defiance of death,
from the gold of your heart's desires,
from the shell of your gloomy self.

4.

Make the self your own.

Decide what is good for you,
learn what is bad for you,
ugly for you, lovely for you:
be your own world.

Drive the sparks out of yourself
from above, from below, from everywhere,
above all, from life's struggle.

GOODNESS

Goodness does not arrive hollering;
it walks quietly, whispering.

Its voice is the voice of suffering,
that has cried for us more than anyone.

Its eyes are quite unhappy,
yet faith and hope shine through.

He wants to offer us what little he has:
they are his pearls, his string of pearls.

They have become heavenly pearls:
he comes not from valleys of the world.

He comes at your darkest moment;
he wants to look into your eyes

to press your hand and go away
as though whispering: it could be better.

LÖYSÄLÄISEN LAULU

Maantietä matkaa
kirjaton, karjaton mies.
Kruununkin kyyti
liika ois hälle kenties,
outoja hälle kun on
isänmaa, kotipaikka ja lies,
puolue, perhe ja muu,
verot, verka ja velka ja ies.

Kuntahan, yhteiskuntahan
kuulumaton,
huonoin hän kansalaisista
kaikista on,
ellei hän kuulunekin
elon varmemman valtiohon,
jonka lie linnat ja maat
liki taivahan auringon.

Mutta hän laulaa! Kuulkaa,
hän kulkeissaan
hyräelee hymysuin
kuin virsiä vierahan maan.
On sanat sekavat. Soi
sorasointuja lauluistaan,
mutta ne näin huminoi
korpehen kohisevaan:

"Vei elon viima mun kukkani.
Jäljelle jäi vain työ
päivien päättymätön,
sydäntuskani talvinen yö.
Järjestykää, polot järjet,
tai Taivahan leimaus lyö:
Miekkoinen nainen ja mies,
ens syksynä leipää ken syö.

DRIFTER'S SONG

Along a country road he travels
a bookless, herdless man.
No doubt, service to the crown
would be too much for him,
since he knows not
fatherland, home or hearth,
political party, family or other,
taxes, debts, yoke or clothing.

Of no community, society
a member,
most wretched of all citizens
is he,
unless he should belong
to the society of ultimate life
whose castles and lands are
near the sun in the sky.

But he sings! Listen,
as he strolls
smiling as he hums
as though hymns of a foreign land.
the words mixed. Discordant notes
he sings,
but they sound like this
in the murmuring forest:

"Life's frost took my flower.
All that remained was work
days unending,
my heartache a winter's night.
Organize, dim-witted wretches,
or heaven's lightning will strike:
Happy-go-lucky man and woman,
who will eat bread next fall?

Vaan mua naurattaa,
mua itkettää iki, ain,
heikkous heltymätön
sanan, vapauden vainoajain.
Minkä he mahtavat?
Pikkuisen piinata vain,
pitkittää, mikö on
kuitenkin täyttymys lain.

Ken? Kuka haastaa?
Tie, elo, totuus ja työ.
Ympäri tauti ja talvi
ja nälkä ja köyhyys ja yö.
Sentään ma, ha, häpeäisin
häntä, ken leipäänsä syö,
kun isän, äidin ja lapsen
ja kullankin kuolema lyö.

Ah, rakas, rakkahin!
Vieläkö kuulet sa mua?
Murheeni huutaa
kuin kaukaista huhuilua.
Muistelen Sua
kuin kaunista kadotettua.
Tuntoni, tuskani määrää
nyt kauas, kauas mun Sua!

Mutta ne vaikka jo vie
minut aallonkin ankaran taa,
missä mun lempeni, lauluni
korkea on kotimaa,
minkä ne mahtavat?
Konsana korkeimpaa
eivät ne nähneet.
Eivätkä nähdä ne saa."

But I have to laugh,
and I have to cry, always,
weakness unrelenting
of word's, freedom's oppressors.
What can they do?
Harass a little bit only,
prolong it, which, however,
is fulfilling the law.

Who? Who summons?
Road, life, truth and work.
Everywhere sickness and winter
and hunger and poverty and night.
Yet I, ah, would be ashamed
of anyone who eats bread
when death strikes his father, mother
and children and even his sweetheart.

Ah, beloved, most beloved!
Do you still hear me?
My sorrow calls
like a far away flute.
I remember You
like a lost beauty.
My feelings, my agony command
me to go far, far from You!

But though they take me away
beyond the grim waves,
from where my homeland is
my love, my song,
what can they do?
Nothing greater
have they seen
nor will ever see."

Maantietä matkaa
kirjaton, karjaton mies.
Maan vai taivahan laps?
Tai helvetin hehkuun on ties!
Outoja sulle kun on
isänmaa, kotipaikka ja lies,
puolue, perhe ja muu:
on sulla sun itsesi ies.

Along a country road he travels
bookless, herdless man.
Child of the earth or sky is he?
Or does his road lead on to hell's fire?
Since you know not
political party, family or other:
you are your own yoke.

NOCTURNE

Ruislinnun laulu korvissani,
tähkäpäiden päällä täysi kuu;
kesä-yön on onni omanani,
kaskisavuun laaksot verhouu.
En ma iloitse, en sure, huokaa;
mutta metsän tummuus mulle tuokaa,
puunto pilven, johon päivä hukkuu,
siinto vaaran tuulisen, mi nukkuu,
tuoksut vanamon ja varjot veen;
niistä sydämeni laulun teen.

Miksi metsän tummuus sävelehen?
Kosk' on mustaa murhe ylpeäin.
Miksi juova päivän laskenehen?
Koska monta nuorta unta näin.
Miksi etäisien vuorten siinto?
Koska sinne oli silmän kiinto.
Miksi vanamoiden valjut lemut?
Koska päättyneet on päivän kemut.
Mutta miksi varjot virran veen?
Kosk' on mieli mulla siimekseen.

Sulle laulan neiti, kesäheina,
sydämeni suuri hiljaisuus,
uskontoni, soipa säveleinä,
tammenlehvä-seppel vehryt, uus.
En ma enää aja virvatulta,
onpa kädessäni onnen kulta;
pienentyy mun ympär' elon piiri;
aika seisoo, nukkuu tuuliviiri;
edessäni hämäräinen tie
tuntemattomahan tupaan vie.

NOCTURNE

Song of a blackbird in my ears,
a full moon above the heads of grain;
happiness of a summer night all mine,
valleys cloaked in smoke of burned-off clearings.
I don't rejoice, don't grieve, sigh;
but bring me darkness of the forest,
glowing cloud into which the sun disappears,
the blue of the windy mountain, which sleeps,
fragrance of twinflowers and shadows over water;
from them my heart a song will make.

Why darkness of the forest in my song?
Because the sorrow of the proud is black.
Why a streak in the day's sunset?
Because my eyes were drawn to them.
Why weak aroma of twinflowers?
Because the day's celebrations now have ended.
But why shadows over waters of a stream?
Because my heart is in the shadow.

To you, maiden, summer grass, do I sing,
my heart a vast stillness,
my faith now rings with melodies,
oak's leafy garland verdant, new.
I no longer chase after will-'o-the-wisps,
in my hand I hold good fortune's gold;
my life's circle grows ever smaller;
time stands still, the weathervane sleeps;
before me a darkening road
that leads to an unknown cottage.

AARO HELLAAKOSKI

AARO HELLAAKOSKI
(1893-1952)

As a young poet, Hellaakoski opposed the then current trend of Finnish poetry—learned, aesthetic expressions of melancholic dreams—and, instead, wrote simple, forceful poetry, often using satire as a weapon. Married to the sister of Finland's greatest sculptor, Väinö Aaltonen, Hellaakoski followed artistic events abroad. He was familiar with German expressionism as well as Apollinaire's experiments in poetry, which he tried, but he never followed one particular school.

Hellaakoski earned a Ph.D. in geology and wrote a number of geological papers. He taught geology as a lecturer at the University of Helsinki and in secondary schools for a number of years. His literary career was marked by two distinct periods, the first one being from 1916 to 1928. He renewed his writing of poetry again in 1943. After World War II his creativity was finally recognized. His poetry revealed his closeness to nature, open attitude toward life, and a sensitive humor. In his later years Hellaakoski was considered to be Finland's greatest living poet, especially by the younger generation of writers whose view of the world paralleled his. Of his many collections, *Jääpeili* (The Ice Mirror, 1928) and *Hiljaisuus* (Stillness, 1949) are considered among his best.

MOONLIGHT IN THE FOREST

Under sleepy branches
a strange light shines,

in the forest a magic path
comes from nowhere, leads nowhere.

My shadow fled. I am
without body. Dissolved into moonlight.

My step remains suspended in mid-air.
My hand touches emptiness.

KUUTAMO METSÄSSÄ

Alla unisen oksiston
valoa kummallista on,

metsän sisällä taikatie
ei mistään tule, ei mihinkään vie.

Varjoni karkasi. Vailla oon
ruumista. Liuonnut kuutamoon.

Askel jää ilmaan irralleen.
Käteni koskee tyhjyyteen.

HAWK

There is room up in the sky.
There is expanse above, below.
The wind hums beneath my wings
and the sun is mine.
Neither hate nor friendship
can touch me,
winter, summer, fall
cannot give me anything;
mine is the only truth, noble
icy cold, eternal.
My eyes did not fail
when I looked into the sun,
my wings did not give out
when I rose above the mountains.
My home is the sky,
my resolve, divinity.
When once I weaken, fall,
from high above I fall.

P. MUSTAPÄÄ

P. MUSTAPÄÄ
(1899-1973)

Martti Haavio, Professor of Finnish and comparative folklore at the University of Helsinki, used the pseudonym P. Mustapää whenever he wrote poetry. He was a versatile stylist and an experimental modernist. He refused to write intellectual poetry, taking his subjects from myths, folktales, ballads, and childish pleasures. His poetry revealed a love of nature and romance, and he wrote with humor and irony.

Among Mustapää's early works are: *Laulu ihanista silmistä* (The Song About the Wonderful Eyes, 1925) and *Laulu Vaakalinnusta* (The Song About the Bird Rukh, 1927). Classical mythology appears in later collections, such as *Ei rantaa ole, oi Thetis* (There Is No Shore, O Thetis, 1948). His last collections are more pessimistic. Some are war poems.

Mustapää received his Ph.D. in 1932. He was a member of the Finnish Academy and became widely known for his studies in folklore and mythology.

46

A MEMORY

What we got, we hardly got in the first place
and what we lost, is hardly gone at all.
The day caressed your temples
and still caresses.
And yet, when I look, night has come
and fog's moistness covers the cape
and yesterday's water-bird
is silent or flown far away.

KANSANSÄVELMÄ

kun läkkiseppä Lindblad soitti
hanurilla tupansa portailla

Vain pieni kansanlaulu,
ja sanoja ei ole ollenkaan,
vain pieni kansanlaulu,
ei sanoja ollenkaan,

vain tuoksua mintun ja ruusun,
jota tuuli kantaa tullessaan,
vain tuoksua mintun ja ruusun
tuo tuuli tullessan,

vain yksinäinen lintu,
joka synkeällä kedolla valittaa,
vain yksinäinen lintu,
joka kedolla valittaa,

vain autius lehtipuissa
ja sininen rakkauden kryytimaa,
vain autius lehtipuissa
sininen, autio maa.

FOLK MELODY

when tinsmith Lindblad played
his accordion on the steps of his cottage

Only a small folk song,
and words there are not any,
only a small folk song,
no words, not any,

only a fragrance of mint and rose,
that the wind brings with it,
only fragrance of mint and rose
the wind brings with it,

only a solitary bird,
who laments in a gloomy field,
only a solitary bird,
who laments in a field,

only desolation in leafy trees
and love's blue garden plot,
only desolation in leafy trees,
blue, desolate land.

A SONG

I wrote a song shining as glass.
Don't think that you can
escape from it. There you will stay
and there always sing.
And the song that I wrote
was without any words:
the most beautiful song I know,
the most beautiful there is.

I wrote a song shining as glass.
Do you now notice, do you sense:
it quietly strengthens
lovely sounds of summer,
babbling of water, movement of oars
and murmur of rushes.

The most beautiful song I know,
the most beautiful song that there is.

LACHESIS NET

In the dimness of the night, summer night,
when pearls of dewdrops fall,
when cobwebs are spun
between leafy branches, among the sedge grass,
when a woodcock runs through the meadow
wings of bats whizzing
wave above black roads,
when an orchestra of birds is playing:
nightjars' resounding cellos,
a dove's tuba, an owl's bass horn,
silver flute of a song thrush,
a grasshopper sat in the summer night
soundless, near the campanula,
in its home pasture, under the rowan trees.

That is when a ball of laughter rolled down to earth:
red and gold and dark
beneath the rowan trees, in the pasture.
That is when a whisper's skein fell:
wool and silk and linen
beneath the rowan trees, in the pasture.

Soundless, near the campanula
sat a grasshopper in wonderment.
The terms he hardly knew, but
the course of thought was clear:
Lachesis net — Kohtalotar* spins.

A graceful maiden, a handsome youth
lingered in the night, summer night,
at home, in the pasture, under the rowan tree.

---

*Goddess or spinner of Fate.

UUNO KAILAS

UUNO KAILAS
(1901-1933)

Uuno Kailas was considered one of the two best poets of Finland during the period between the wars, and he was a member of the *Tulenkantajat* (Torch Bearers), whose objective was to lead the way for Finnish literature by bringing in the light of European literary traditions.

Kailas was the prototype of the tragic poet: no money, poor physical and mental health, and early death from tuberculosis. He wrote metaphysical poetry, emphasized the search for truth, and worked toward self-improvement. He was, in fact, abnormally self-centered and his poetry reflects his subconscious terrors. Kailas never married nor had any children.

In his second collection of poetry, *Purjehtijat* (The Seafarers, 1925), Kailas came closest to the spirit of the *Tulenkantajat* in the use of free verse and exotic imagery. *Silmästä silmään* (From Eye to Eye, 1926) made him well known. It shows his progressive turn inward. The thought of death obsessed Kailas and became more apparent in his later collections. In *Uni ja Kuolema* (Sleep and Death, 1931) his personality reaches its culmination.

Kailas was also a translator and a critic. In 1926 he published an anthology of German poetry that he had translated into Finnish (from Goethe to contemporary poets).

IN A SMALL COUNTRY

Boundaries too small. No space in which to step.
Everyone here is in everyone else's way and bites one another.
Every neighbor at his gate attacks unexpectedly
secret grudge and envy—dog, lurking for bones.

Boundary lines everywhere. And at gates, signs:
"This is my territory," and "Turn back!"
They measure the air by cubic inches for each other:
here, breathe this—now stop breathing!

PIENESSÄ MAASSA

Rajat liian pienet. Ei ole askelen alaa.
Kukin täällä on muiden tiellä ja puree muita.
Joka naapuriportista hyöppää arvaamatta
salakauna ja kateus—koira, väijyvä luita.

Raja-aitoja kaikkialla. Ja porteilla kilpi:
"Tämä on minun alueeni" ja "Käänny tästä!"
He mittaavat kuutiotuumin ilman toisillensa:
kas, hengitä tämä—ja lakkaa hengittämästä!

MY SON

My son—unborn
only dreamed of—,
this moment so quiet
you near me in my cottage.

Against the edge of my work table
I see your chin, little man.
You have already been there a while
or even longer, perhaps.

Your large child's eyes
clear as a brook, look at me.
Your helpless hand
you extend toward me.

You say quietly the word: Father.
Nothing more.
When I want to grasp your hand,
it suddenly disappears.

But as though invisible
it seems to invite me: This way!
—My son, in your eyes
I see my own immortality,

the only thing that remains
when my body has decayed,
and because of that immortality
I love you.

I know: when Death
takes me toward Emptiness,
if I will then feel
your small fingers in my hands

and if, son, you still say
a small word, quietly,
I won't be afraid to join
the circle of Nonexistence, no.

GUILTY MAN

He will be shot. He is a guilty man.

He looks silently at us and away from us.
He gives his eyes to me and commands: look!
And then I see who is also a guilty man.

Guilt's ring of iron is on the wrists of us all.
Guilt's indebted slaves are we, chained to him.
And the army of our conscience surrounds us.

But one of us has broken death's circle.
I see how he sheds his soiled clothes.
From the shadow of guilt's wings he steps into the light.

I see his new countenance: he is the robber on the cross,
he is my brother, the guilty man, who will be shot.

THE HOUSE

My house was built in just one night—
through whose efforts, the Lord only knows.
—Did he help, the Black Carpenter
in setting up the timbers?—

My house is cold,
windows toward the night.
Ice-cold embers of despair,
the fire on my hearth.

No friend, no visitor
need come.
There is no door for them.
Only two doors have I,
Two: to sleep and to death.

KATRI VALA

KATRI VALA
(1901-1944)

Katri Vala was born into a literary family and started writing poetry at eleven. Her first collection, *Kaukainen puutarha* (The Faraway Garden, 1924), won the literary prize of the government. Vala became an enthusiastic member of the *Tulenkantajat* (Torch Bearers), a group of young writers. She, together with other young writers, published an anthology, *Hurmoituneet kasvot* (The Rapturous Face, 1925); its intention was to capture the essence of the *Tulenkantajat* outlook. In the late 'twenties, two of Vala's collections were published.

In 1928 she learned that she had tuberculosis. She was able to marry and to bear a child, but her philosophy and art were modified both by her illness and by the environment where she lived in Helsinki. Her observations of suffering during the deep depression years and the brutalities of the developing Fascist movement prompted her to side with the workers' movement and with the pacifists—for humanitarian rather than political reasons.

Vala's writing style and subject matter began to change with her new social awareness. Her early collections had expressed passionate joy of life, an unquenchable thirst for all sensuous pleasures. In *Paluu* (Return, 1934) she abandoned her old style and began to write more concisely about the poor, about injustice, oppression and violence.

She died in 1944 in Sweden, where she had gone for medical treatment after publishing her last book, *Pesäpuu palaa* (The Nesting Tree Burns, 1942). In 1945 her ashes were brought home and were buried with honors by the Finnish government.

STRING OF PEARLS

I am but a little girl
before your passionate eyes,
whose gaze burns more than all your caresses.

Only a sorrowful heart
have I to give,
but my shadow glides enchanted
above your feet.

Silenced by love
I look at your face,
oh, my black god,
and like a red jewelry box
my heart conceals days and nights,
a string of pearls
that you gave me.

But if tired of me,
you close your eyes,
I'll vanish more quietly
than stars from morning sky.

THE CHILD PLAYS

It's raining outside, the child is talking.
It's so nice to be here.
Let's play, Mother, our home is the world
at the bottom of the sea.
The water around us is crystal and quiet.

Your hands, Mother, are two pretty fish
that play with me gently,
your voice, Mother,
is the silver bell in the blue tower
that rings over the meadow of the sea.

The bookshelf is a wise cliff
where there are a thousand golden eyes.
All the vases are shells,
sea's loveliest ears that hum.
And the lamp, oh Mother, is a brightly lit ship
that glides, rocking above our world.
I long to board that ship—

SILTA

Oi että sydämeni olisi horjumaton kallio,
mutta minä värisen taakkani alla.

Maailman kaikilta ääriltä
tarttuvat käsiini lasten pelokkaat kädet,
sydämeni seinät vavahtelevat
miljoonain tuskan huudosta,
minä, ihmisen rakastaja,
vapisen syntymän edessä,
koska se on kärsimyksen syntymä.
Oi että olisin väkevä kuin meri,
voisin kaataa laulullani muurin,
joka erottaa teidät elämän
päivännousumaasta.
Mutta minä olen vain hauras silta,
jonka yli tienne kulkee.

THE BRIDGE

If only my heart were an unwavering rock,
but I tremble beneath my burden.

From all parts of the world
children's frightened hands reach out to mine,
walls of my heart almost burst
when I hear the agonized cries of millions,
I, who love people,
shake in the presence of birth
because it is the birth of suffering.
If only I were strong as the sea
with my song I could push down the wall
that separates you from life's sunrise.
But I am only a shaky bridge
over which your road must go.

WINTER HAS COME

Winter has come again—

If I were young,
perhaps I would sing
of the earth's black bowl
filled with coolness of snowflowers,
perhaps dew of the stars
my song would sparkle on night's blue meadow.

But the songs of my youth are frozen.
My song is poor and weary,
like a wife
who, with knotted blue hands,
gathers twigs
for the fire in her humble home.

I circle the meager bread line,
grim as a prison yard,
my senses, thoughts both dulled by work.

Winter has come,
intensifying misery,
lashing children of poverty
with its frosty whip.
But rowan trees flame
like beacons.

YRJÖ JYLHÄ

YRJÖ JYLHÄ
(1903-1956)

Yrjö Jylhä is best known for his Finnish classic, *Kiirastuli* (Purgatory, 1941), a profound poetic work based on his experiences as commander of an infantry company during the Winter War. Many of his other collections, as well as their titles, reveal his concept of the world as a constant struggle, both spiritual and physical, as in *The Whirlpool, In the Cage of the Tiger*, and *The Galley Slave*.

His many skilled translations include *Paradise Lost*, stories by Cervantes, Heine's *Buch der Lieder*, and works of Shakespeare, Milton, and Wordsworth. He studied at the University of Helsinki and was a member of the group of young writers, *Tulenkantajat* (Torch Bearers).

70

HOLY NIGHT

There was a man named Jooseppi Kirvesmies,
who was where we all were;
he, too, had left his home and wife,
and the weeks and months went by.
He seldom wrote to Marjatta
and seldom got a letter;
on the night of Christmas Eve, when the firing
had let up, sparing our thinning numbers,
we all could hear together:

A son is born to Jooseppi
and Marjatta, and Marjatta!
Born beneath the blackest beam,
with scarcely a cover for Him—

In spirit, we all knelt down,
bowed before the Child,
with reverence we adored Him.

Many bearded shepherds stayed watch,
protecting the holy Infant
throughout the snowy night
from those who would betray Him,
and the earth and heavens rang out in praise.

A star shone bright above the Finnish forests,
a star larger than all the others,
and together we turned to look;
in our minds it brought us home,
the star larger than all the others.

KOHTAUS METSÄSSÄ

Kiväärinpiippu ja silmää kaksi
sua väijyvät rävähtämättä,
sinä surmanliekin laukaisijaksi
kohotat kättä.

Vain silmänräpäys, hyytävä hetki`
ja pitkä kuin iankaikkisuus:
joko päättyy sult' elon partioretki,
joko metsään maatuvat luus?

on hällä oikeus tappaa, ja sulla—
mut mistä saitte sen oikeuden?
Ei voi hän vieraaksi majaas tulla:
hän on vihollinen.

Et tiedä ken on hä, mistä,
et tiedä hänestä muuta,
kuin että käy joku ihmisistä
päin pistoolinsuuta.

Niin kohtaavat toisensa länsi ja itä,
niin kohtaavat ihmiset toisiaan.
Vain toinen muistelemaan jäi sitä,
ja toista jossakin kaivataan.

A MEETING IN THE FOREST

A rifle barrel and a pair of eyes
watching you without blinking,
as discharger of death's flame
you raise your hand.

Only a blinking of an eye, blood-curdling moment
and long as eternity:
is your life's reconnaissance coming to an end,
will your bones moulder in the forest?

He has the right to kill, as do you—
but where did you get that right?
He cannot come to your home as a guest:
he is the enemy.

You don't know who he is, from where,
you know nothing about him
except that a human being
will face the pistol's fire.

Thus they meet, East and West,
thus people meet each other.
But one is left to remember,
the other somewhere is mourned.

MORE

I yearn to be more than I am:
ruler of the earth that I humbly trod,
master of myself, also a guide for others,
comfort to those whose hearts are heavy.

I yearn to do more than I do,
forge stars into the darkness,
conjure flowers into the mud and the soil,
cover earth's filth with pearls and gold.

I yearn to see more clearly than I see:
hurl through the night, a glowing spark,
tear open gods' secrets,
know the old and interpret the new.

I yearn to go farther than I go
to the gate where you see eternity,
unfasten the fetters of relentless time,
glide away, cleansed, across the divide.

ARVO TURTIAINEN

ARVO TURTIAINEN
(1904-1980)

Arvo Turtiainen, the grand old man of Finnish poetry, was unusually successful in keeping up with the times. A central figure in left-wing literature, he was a member of *Kiila* (The Wedge), the leftest writers' group, and its director for 18 years. He fought for his country in the Winter War and was wounded, but was imprisoned as a pacifist during the Continuation War.

His earliest poetry appeared in 1936, declamatory poetry in free verse about everyday life in an industrial city. In 1939, *Tie pilven alta* (Under the Cloud and Away, 1939) appeared, containing epitaphs to workers and simple people who suffered or died prematurely during the Civil War, with whom Turtiainen identified perhaps more strongly than any other proletarian poet in Finland.

A new phase in his work became evident in his collections *Minä rakastan* (I Love, 1955) and *Syyskevät* (Autumn Spring, 1959). His poetry became more personal in tone and he began to include social satire. *Minä paljasjalkainen* (Born and Bred in Helsinki, 1962) brought him to the notice of a large readership as the chronicler of the past and present of Helsinki. In 1974, his collection, *Leivän kotimaa* (The Homeland of Bread), was published, and in 1976 a large collection of his poetry, *Runoja 1934-1968* (Poems 1934-1968), came out.

Among works translated into Finnish by Turtiainen are Masters' *Spoon River Anthology*, Whitman's *Leaves of Grass*, Mayakovski's *A Cloud in the Trousers*, and poems by Pasternak. He was awarded State Prizes for poetry in 1955 and 1962 and for translations in 1970. Throughout his long life, Turtiainen remained a committed and innovative poet.

76

SHOEMAKER NIKKE

(Childhood memory)

1

He cared about us children,
we often gathered near his footstool
and watched how he pulled the waxed thread
with his thin, long-boned fingers.
Then he would pause in his work
and take part in our play.
Once, I remember it well,
we sat in a circle, in the shade of an elder bush.
Shoemaker Nikke leaned forward on his knees and said *ugh*.
He was Sitting Bull
and we his brave red-skinned tribe.

2

Not until the day
when the first shots rang out
near the edge of the city, not until then
did Shoemaker Nikke reach for his rifle.
(I am a man of peace, he said often,
I do not approve of war.)
But that day
he stepped outside in front of the old woman,
he had a red ribbon and a rifle
and he spoke. He spoke about
us us us and about
how the world would change.
One of the old women wept, someone said:
Nikke, a rifle doesn't suit you.

We children stood stiffly near him,
we were a bit afraid, the rifle scared us,
but we thought Nikke was marvelous that day.

Then that summer I saw how prisoners were transported.
They trudged forward in a long line,
broken men, thin, bearded faces.
It was hot, the sun glowed
and the dust cloud from their feet
spread the stench from their dirty rags.
That's when I remembered Nikke, thought of him
and all the others, thought:
Are these the same men who in the winter
had a red ribbon and a rifle?

And one day it was announced
that Nikke had died,
died of hunger, they said, like a dog,
he wasn't even shot.
We children were subdued for many days,
sneaked out to the elder bush, but no one
felt like playing, no one said *ugh*.
We sat there in the sun blinking our eyes,
we didn't say much, we didn't smile,
only sat there
like a bevy of clumsy, broken-winged birds.
The sun shone, Nikke was dead.

THAT DAY THE RECORD OF 130 MILES WAS BROKEN

And the same day a shoemaker,
one who died of hunger,
was lowered into the arms of the grave.

AND THE WINNER, DANDY FOREIGNER, DROVE IN A CIRCLE DAZED BY THE ACCLAIM

The shoemaker's coffin was cracked,
the only escort his widow.

WHEN THE RACE WAS OVER,
ABOVE THE NOISE OF THE CROWD
A VOICE ON THE LOUDSPEAKER RANG OUT:
—DEAR SPECTATORS, TECHNOLOGY,
THE VICTORY OF INTELLECT,
LEADS THE HUMAN RACE FORWARD

But a sandy grave
quite nearby
was the shoemaker's humble destination.
He lived and died
with hardship
and testified: progress non-existent.

KAUNEIN

Kaunein runo syntyy
kun ihminen on lähellä ihmistä,
kun hellyys,
yksinkertainen ja rajaton,
vailla kysymyksiä
virtaa toisesta toiseen.

Kauneinta runoa ei unohda.
Se on sinetöity otsaan, silmiin,
huuliin ja sydämeen,
sinetöity rakastavien lukea,
rakastavien kirvoittaa.

LOVELIEST POEM

The loveliest poem is born
when you are close to someone,
when tenderness,
simple and boundless,
without questions
flows from one to the other.

You do not forget the loveliest poem.
It is stamped on your forehead, eyes,
lips and heart,
stamped for lovers to read,
for lovers to surrender.

BALLAD OF HERMAN'S ROSE

Helsinki

Granite
in the hands, waves of the sea,
mussels, in the hollows of your wide roots.
The sea pushes you toward the land, the land toward the sea,
your fishermen do not support you,
    they have died,
their cottages, boats buried on your shores,
        underneath smoky-gray flowers.
In the cold chasms of gravel, brick and cement.

But yet your are beautiful, your summers beautiful
as the sun sets on your shores.
Hilly streets, towers, factory chimneys,
people on the streets, markets, parks.
They continue to repeat: Helsinki, Helsinki!
    their own, those
who know where they came from, where they were born,
    not knowing
that you were no longer, you are not yet
since you were destroyed, burned, disappeared
into the flames of sunrises, sunsets of my childhood,
    when those
who know where they have come from,
rushed to build you.

You are coming, Helsinki,
again coming
into the vanishing dreams
of your children and children's children.

I

There where the Kulo Saari bridge
arches over gleaming green waters,
a landscape where the chimneys of the Arabia factory
thrust their spearheads into the heart of the morning sun,
there where ships glide
ocean's salt spatterings on their masts
in the warm tar smell of the pier, there
where the oil rushes in the pipes, winches squeaking
and stevedores shouting and terns shrieking
as they drum against the sky above the sound, there
in the shade of the prison wall,
dock workers playing cards behind a pile of lumber
and drivers selling whiskey in stable yards,
there by an alley
where widows of Red Guards* raised their children
singing hymns and biting their lips,
there where Rose was born one night
as drunken sailors staggered toward their ships
and as one of them sang a tune
that was cold and hot at the same time,
like silver coins that a man gives to a woman
in payment for love
that you can never get for money.

III

Where could I find the words
to tell correctly about all of this?
Should I ask Rose, Rose herself
how she got
mixed up in all this?

She was sixteen
and worked at the Arabia porcelain factory.
For her work, her hands,
she was paid three marks an hour;

* The opposing sides in the Finnish Civil War of 1918 are traditionally called the White Guards (the official established government) and the Red Guards (the socialists).

rather than mixing clay,
her graceful hands
should have been molded in clay, her fingers
worn by the clay,
should have been fingerlings swimming in brooks,
flying free as birds.
Should I ask her eyes, pupils
that shine like flames
in the garden she created,
like stones that have been rubbed into pearls
                              by gleaming waters
in the transparent deepness of a green current,
her eyes, that were created
not to stare at clay
but to bathe in their own beauty,
to invite others to bathe
in her transparent waters?

Should I ask her body,
her swaying walk,
that was like a ship on the high seas in full sail,
her hips, that were like two oval waves,
her ankles, around which bells jangled,
an invitation to dance?

She was sixteen
when all this started,
her age immaterial
when it ended.

She is no more,
the flame in her eyes
is gone, the pearls
totally covered.

She is no more,
the waves of her body
died in the waste waters
of the Old City bay.

V

Finally I understood Rose's death
and that of my youth in Helsinki
together with hers.

I released
my stiffened fingers
from the nostrils of the wind.

Go! I said to the wind.
Awaken her sisters to mourn,
howl in her brothers' ears.

Drive her lover
to wade
in her blood!

The wind snorted
and rose to its feet.
The wind attacked in all directions.

It shook the prison gates,
it rattled factory windows,
it pounded tin roofs with its fists
to awaken the conscience of the people.

Never again! howled the wind as it traveled.
Never ever again!
I know of a salve for your wounds.

> This black stone
> I cut for your crown
> city.

Jofa köyhä armahtaa,
hän laihnaa HErralle;
jofa hänen hywän työn-
fä hänelle fällen maffa-
wa on. Sananlaffu
Kirian. 2.19. v.17.
1845

VILJO KAJAVA

VILJO KAJAVA
(1909-   )

Viljo Kajava has had a remarkably long career as a poet, and he was writing about the "problems of proletarian poetry" before the formation in 1936 of the leftist writers' group *Kiila* (The Wedge). He considered early proletarian poetry too general and rhetorical and called for a graphic description of individual cases. His first two poetry collections, *Rakentajat* (The Builders, 1935) and *Murrosvuodet* (The Years of the Crisis, 1937), are his most radical.

Kajava studied at the University of Helsinki and was at first a member of the young literary group *Tulenkantajat* (Torch Bearers) before joining *Kiila*. He broke with *Kiila* during World War II and began writing poetry inspired by events of the time. He lived in Sweden during the late 'forties where he became acquainted with contemporary Swedish poetry and published two collections in Swedish. On returning to Finland, his new Finnish collections had considerable influence on the new poetry then developing.

In the 'sixties, Kajava renewed an interest in social and political themes. His collection, *Tampereen runot* (Poems of Tampere, 1966), deals with his hometown, the most important industrial city in Finland, and the Civil War of 1918, during which Tampere suffered considerably. Another work, *Käsityöläisenunet* (Dreams of a Craftsman, 1968), includes reflections on workers' conditions and invocations of peace. One section is dedicated to Lorca.

Today his poems, with their subtly changing moods and thoughts, are reminiscent of Chinese poetry. In 1980 he published his 33rd poetry collection. He was awarded the State Prize for poetry in 1954, 1966 and 1977.

I AM A GUITAR

I am a guitar
made from a red, warm tree.
I am a wall
against which the guitar breaks.
I am the man
who breaks the guitar.

I am the event
where the guitar's red flame dies,
I am the gestalt above the event
that for a moment flares into life,
I am the silence
after the event
and I disappear into it.

FATHER IS LEAVING

Five o'clock, grey dawn in February.
Mother awakened sister and me: Father is leaving.
The rifle stock bumped against the doorpost.
A kiss for mother,
we two for a moment in Father's lap,
the look in his brown eyes
over all of us,
sound of the rifle stock on the wooden steps.
Thus he left.

Mother's thin fists pounded the boards
of the closed kitchen door.

from SONGS OF SORROW (*Spring 1918*)

Torn widow's veil
and through it, still, bloody thorns.
One thorn under the wedding ring,
memory's sharp scar.

Wading through April's snowy sludge
the horse carried its rider
saddlebags, heavy with ammunition, hitting its flanks.
April in the bristle of the rider's beard,
hunger and emptiness in his eyes,
as the horse and the man traveled toward defeat.

Gray hoarfrost of Pispala Road on the horse's nose.
Gray in the beard of the man on the horse.
Then the saddlebags discarded by the wayside,
lunch bag held close to his thin chest
as the April gray horse and the man with April's sludge
within him
traveled toward defeat.

Who knows what bird it was
that came to the city in May
when the trees had burned down in the gunfire
when people's glances dimmed toward each other.
What was that bird
that I heard in May?
It was a sound I heard
when I pressed my head againt my mother's wrist.

* * *

When I was very little the lake was blue,
and the stones on the shore were warm.
When I was very little
mother's arm smelled of morning,
when I was very little
I walked from dream to dream
on all fours.

* * *

The sky went before me wherever I went,
over blue mountain, over heather,
and even where the water began, the sky went before me,
and when finally I looked back
there was still sky left behind me,
quite a bit of sky was still left behind me.

* * *

Rain's small cool fingers
carefully dig up a blue flower from the soil;
the sky, whose cloud has
my loving grandmother's shape,
wraps the newborn in its lacy covers

* * *

LOVE IS NOT CLEANSED BY FIRE

Love is not cleansed by fire
          nor by needless sacrifices,
love is tried on gray ordinary days
moments of weariness, in deadening work.

The imaginary bride in poetry
twists her gold ring
in her infinite, idle loneliness,—
but true love is near
where a man praises his wife's worn, wrinkled
          hands in the poor light of a night lamp
          as sleep approaches.

EEVA- LIISA MANNER

EEVA-LIISA MANNER
(1921-   )

Eeva-Liisa Manner is a significant figure in Finnish literature and regarded by some as the most international of Finnish poets. She is a philosophical poet, her lyricism charged with implications. Her poems reflect a deep feeling for music and a special interest in mythology. The influence of oriental philosophy is also evident.

Her fourth collection, *Tämä Matka* (This Journey, 1956), became the most influential book of poetry for the Finnish modernist movement of the 'fifties and established her as a leading poet of that period.

She has also excelled as a playwright, novelist and translator. She has translated Homer's *Iliad* and the words of Shakespeare, Ben Johnson, Herman Hesse, and Oscar Parland. She is the recipient of numerous State Prizes for poetry, drama and translations.

Manner lived in Spain for several years, and in two of her collections Spanish motifs are evident: *Kirjoitettu Kivi* (The Written Rock, 1966) and *Fahrenheit 121* (1968). A more recent work, *Kuolleet vedet* (Dead waters: cycles on public and private mythologies, 1977), is a fine introspective collection by this respected Finnish modernist. A wide selection of her poems were published under one cover in 1980: *Runoja 1956-1977* (Poems 1956-1977).

96

HERE

How loneliness spreads from me,
bushes die away,
trees flee and martens, and martens.
Night's coldness moves slowly farther away
        like the edge of a glacier
and covers small bodies.
Trees on the outside carry emptiness,
loneliness
like a stone moves from tree to tree.
Endlessness

and snow.

TÄÄLLÄ

Miten yksinäisyys minusta leviää,
pensaat kuolevat pois,
puut pakenevat ja naadat, ja naadat.
Yön kylmyys työntyy hitaasti kauemmaksi
        kuin jäätikön reuna
ja peittää pienet ruumiit.
Puut ulkopuolella tyhjyyttä kannattavat,
yksinäisyys
niin kuin kivi puulta puulle siirtyy.
Äärettömyyttä

ja lunta.

INTO THE SILENCE OF THE FOREST

I am like a foolish elk
who sees her reflection in the water
and thinks that she has drowned.

Or what does she think?
Perhaps she sees another elk there.

But there is not that much difference.
I must become what I am
and not what I think I am
or what I would like to be;
nor, either, that which you are (or the other one);

this becoming of mine is a slow disrobing:
to leave the clothing of my individuality
on the common shore and to swim,

always I must swim across, always toward the other shore;
already I once saw my cloak of anonymity
                        climb up a steep precipice
and disappear into the silence of the forest, never returning.

ASSIMILATION

I will show you a way
that I have travelled

if you come
if you come back some day
searching for me

do you see how everything shifts a little every moment
and becomes less pretentious and more primitive
(like pictures drawn by children
or early forms of life: the soul's alphabet)

you will come to a warm region
it is soft and hazy
but then I will no longer be me,

but the forest.

A WALK

That year spring came very late
We walked along hard echoing roads
The trees turned slowly toward evening

Trees, earth, day and all natural signs
Continually there was light somewhere, or was it snow
We talked of many things, and I

showed you my heart,
also that room where no one has ever come
I felt a solemn melancholy

The leaves had not yet opened
Ideas in the bud, the tree large and empty
only a bird chirped its non-musical idea

We parted, and I wandered continually in that tree
through the dark and tranquil village of my sleep
                              and snow fell from somewhere
and a bird kept chirping, and is repeating still

SPECULATION

This is how I die a little every day
(the more I love, the more do I die),
until I receive the mercy of the dead: I no longer
need to die.

And a world that changes a little every day
constantly loses human qualities:
(mountains look more and more like mountains, seas like seas),
water doesn't remember, doesn't forget, doesn't reflect the sky,
the sky is an illusion in my eyes, and water is water.

BACH

There is a stream,
stones that arrange into bridges,
engraved dragons sleep golden under water,
stairs to climb to many white houses,
revered, to the remains of Bruno, to Pascal's
                              polyphonic reflections,
rest and freedom in Giotto's deep blueness

Arrested time
builds a city,
within which is another city,
bridges within which are other bridges
for snow white horses and holy donkeys;
stairs, echoes transmitting space, everything perfect;

donkeys with haloes; painful nailed hooves
fall off and flower into seven-edged lilies
that you created
for angels to kiss—

donkeys with haloes, a golden plate,
ten keys on each plate,
like divine fingers
that weave music from light and water

And gates open   open
purple flowers open, they are a variation and a flute,
discarded wings open, rise high, are a fugue,
the towers tremble, locked cities of shedding doves
are an intimate mosiac, and here

LAST YEAR IN CAPRICORN

Stairs, echoes,
mirrors, stairs,
echoes, mirrors,
footprints gleam in the dust,
echoing space, light
deep within the mirror.
And sky blue hides the rusty gate,
summer, winter, summer
it flowers delicately, sky blue,
and above the yard swallows weave
their noisy net.

Rooms, echoes,
echoes (distant as though one's ear were
very far from the floor),
in the mirror another empty
illuminated room
(as though hollowed into cold crystal)

and above the hermetically sealed space sped a shy lizard
and in the dust the footprints still gleamed
and from the newly cut hayfield came a whistle
and in the jasmine a bird answered
and the flowers shed their petals incessantly.

FROM MY LIFE I MAKE A POEM

From my life I make a poem, from a poem a life,
a poem is a way to live and the only way to die
with ecstatic indifference:
glide into infinity, drift
at God's level for a special weightless moment,
level with God's cold eyes,

that do not weep, do not stay awake, do not form opinions,
watch with disinterest, favoring everything,
pursue order and strictly scheduled moments,
protect scorpions, snakes, cuttle-fish
(which humans hate, confusing these forms
with their own passions);

a poem acknowledges one religion: Curiosity,
wander through the habitats of Pisces, Scorpio and Capricorn,
Borrowing from a bird desire and flight
and floats down
    like a wing wrapped in the wind,
swift freedom, like a bird.

ANJA VAMMELVUO

ANJA VAMMELVUO
(1921-   )

Anja Vammelvuo, who has had a long, productive literary career, has been compared with Katri Vala, whose work she admires. Her first collection of poetry, *Auringon Tytär* (The Daughter of the Sun, 1943), was very personal, but as her writing developed, she revealed a deep concern for the problems of individuals and society, as in *Kukkia sylissäni* (Flowers In My Lap, 1954).

Vammelvuo's two main themes, love and humanism, are prominent in her poetry. She continues to defend the right to life and freedom. Important to her is the destiny of women. In her poems, women are never submissive or passive. Her collection, *Totuuden iskut* (Truth's Blows, 1973), deals with love and the joy of living, but also includes poems that are politically oriented—straightforward affirmations, even vehement stands, for what she believes and supports. Her experience has been wide and is reflected in her writing. The timeliness of her poetry has assured her continued support. In 1981 a large selection of her poems (1947-1977) were published.

Vammelvuo received a degree from the University of Helsinki in 1941 and has been the recipient of three State Prizes for poetry.

SMALL BOYS

Small boys broke off from us
every spring
small boys big guns,
big guns small boys.

Prepare your heart, woman.
With eyelids closed look again
far away vastness of snow in morning dimness
boys, boys wading
crouching in cold snow.

Rifles, rifles extending
vastness of snow farther than the eye can see.

ALEKSANDRA KOLLONTAY*

As though my own mother had died.
Through the rumble of busses, clanging of cans,
                              through the sun
I tell women: our mother has died.

In the morning when the sun is up

blue overalls multi-colored scarves
come down in a hurry

They heard the sad news, I know,
concealed it in their distress,
accustomed to moving forward.

No one has died
when the sun is up.
Whoever looks back
belongs to death.

An internationally known Russian feminist as well as diplomat and novelist, Alexandra Kollantay served as Soviet Ambassador to Sweden from 1930-1945. In 1944 she helped conduct peace negotiations for the Soviet-Finnish Armistice. She died in 1952.

ANOTHER SPRING, ANOTHER YEAR

I am spending this evening with you.
You are in the urn on the mantel.
That is against the law.
You are the flower in the goblet
from which we drank a festive cognac,
on the radio violin music, I don't recognize it.

a chill—
I could hardly make it to the table.
Your stern picture on the shelf has tipped on its side.
Your eyes bored a hole in my breast.

Another spring.
Another year.
You are in this cottage.
You son phoned.
Today it is twenty-five years
since you took me to Mehiläinen
an overnight bag in my hand.
Tomorrow our child will be born, again.

EVEN THE MIRROR DIES

When I lived here in the shade of your love,
you loved every small object around me,
you brought them, you rejoiced when I played.

Now they are all going away from me
                              in a steady stream.
There is no room for any of them.
My life is being shoved into cellars and attics.

Now I remember my mother and that dreadful china cabinet
which we scorned and laughingly gave away for a dime,
killed my mother's way of life, gold-edged, beveled glass doors.

Now I am being swept away.
My big, tremendous life
does not fit into the world.
Even the mirror dies when you
do not stand behind me and, with your hands, say
which lines in me you love.

AILA MERILUOTO

AILA MERILUOTO
(1924-   )

Aila Meriluoto was 22 when she published her first poetry collecton, *Lasimaalaus* (Glass Painting), in 1946. Except for Väinö Linna's war classic, *Tuntematon Sotilas* (The Unknown Soldier), it is the most sensational work ever published in Finland. Young critics and conservative scholars alike praised it for its timeliness and its merits. Particularly quoted was her poem "Kivinen Jumala" (The Stone God), since all readers identified with its protest against the horrors of the war that had just ended.

Meriluoto's subsequent collections have been well received, confirming her place among Finland's leading poets. *Sairas tyttö tanssii* (The Sick Girl Dances, 1956) and *Asumattomiin* (Deserted Places, 1963), in which she writes of loneliness more objectively than in previous poetry, are among the later collections. In *Elämästä* (About Life, 1972) and *Varokaa putoilevia enketeitä* (Watch Out for Falling Angels, 1977) she continues with her quietly sensitive, openly subjective style. In 1980 she published *Talvikaupunki* (Winter City), her tenth and perhaps most important work so far—controlled, undemonstrative, and rich in imagery.

Meriluoto has translated the works of Rainer Maria Rilke, whom she acknowledges as a main influence. She also translated into Finnish the work of Harry Martinson.

Meriluoto earned a University degree in 1943. She was awarded State Prizes for poetry in 1946 and 1962 and one for translations in 1974.

THE STONE GOD

God, I pound and I pound and I pound,
begging, blaspheming, praying I pound.
Open Your gate, open, open!
Open Your eyes, Unmoving!
See: a thousand mothers loving
protecting their crying children
as walls fall down and roofs collapse.
World filled with oppression and terror.
Their tears dig furrows into their souls,
eternal furrows, deep and bitter . . .
With broken fists I pound.

Who are You? In terror I see You:
an unmoving stone head,
proud nostrils not breathing,
a stone mouth, two hands of stone,
eyes—oh not that, have mercy, help!
empty blind eyes like a grave.
Stone God, devoid of life.
There is, there is no savior.

I clutch your hands, sister and brother.
Mute, we rise from the ruins.
Desolate world, somber as a well.
All is the same, whether we die or live.
Yet we rise from the ruins,
yet we rise, stone dominion,
in our breasts a stony defiance and rage,
we rise with no faith, no mercy,
we rise with no tomorrow.
Mute, we rise, faces hardened,
faces of stone, breasts of stone,
like our God of stone.

For long we believed in purposeless sleep.
Night had fallen over the people,
eternal darkness avenged the sun.
God raised his stone face.
But we grew in the darkness,
we too of stone, we too of night,
truth sat on our shoulders like a load of granite.
Stone God, You awakened us.
In Your own image You made us.
Cold we stand, until tomorrow.

IN THE YEAR 4 AFTER FATHER

You came already the first summer
when Irja was doing her exercises upstairs
and I was in the pantry secretly eating cheese:
steps on the veranda, heavy, typical
(your boots were always a bit too big).
The following summer the dog knew it,
growled from the porch into the empty cottage,
                    lifted his nose
and wagged his tail to the one approaching, pausing,
                          on the stairs, on the way up.
Now it is only joy, deeper than I ever realized.
You transcend boundaries.
Thus we repeat ourselves
from generation to generation.

RANNALLA

Paljain jaloin rannalla
kun aamu on harmaan kiven alla
ja tahto litistynyt kuin kärpänen
mustat rippeet ja valkoista tahmaa.
Miksi aina vain haavoittua
ei terävään vaan tylsään:
pyöreihin kiviin jotka painuvat jalkapohjan lihaan
pyöreihin sanoihin jotka eivät leikkaa mitään
aamuihin kotka jäävät rähmäälleen.
Haavoittua ilman haavaa, ilman verta
vain häipyvä valkoinen jälki, valkoinen sylki
kärpäsen sisälmykset.

Kiveä harmaampi on meri,
meri vapahtaja, meri puhtaaksipesijä,
meri ihana, ainoa jolla on voima ja kunnia olla
vain välinpitämätän.

ON THE SHORE

Barefoot on the shore
when morning is under a gray stone
and will is squashed like a fly,
black anchors and white slime.
Why always get wounded
not by sharp but by dull:
round stones that press into the
                          soles of my feet
round words that do not cut anything
mornings that remain flat.
Wounded without a word, without blood
only a fading white mark, white spittle
a fly's insides.

The sea is grayer than the stone,
sea the savior, sea the cleanser,
sea the beautiful, only thing that has
                  the honor and power to be
but indifferent.

I LOOK AT YOUR LAND

Dear Father (heavenly),
I look at Your land from the upstairs window.
We sold the shore trees when we had to fix
                    the sauna roof,
now you can see the lake all the way across:
how small it is.
Just as small as forty years ago
when the gentry came to look at the old tenant farm house
(to buy it if it pleased them)
and the tenant farmer's children stood in the rye field, frightened
 eye to eye with the children of the gentry
                    who looked elsewhere:
no trees anywhere, empty, windy,
don't Father buy this.
The children stepped out of the way,
of course something did grow,
we planted trees, used logs for siding.
Mature trees, sold,
the sky changes.
Is this what I will leave my children: polluted lake,
decaying logs, brush to burn.
Someone else gives the sky.

HELENA ANHAVA

HELENA ANHAVA
(1925-   )

Originally a writer of prose, Helena Anhava appeared as a new poetic voice in 1971 with her collection of poems, *Murheellisen kuullen on puhuttava hiljaa* (Among the Grieving One Should Speak Softly). Since then she has published five more collections. Her poems, which are intimate and reflective, have attracted a large readership. They deal with everyday events, human relations, nature, maternal love, the problems of children, and the right of young people to grow up naturally. Her book *Hidas osa* (Slow Movement, 1979) was awarded the 1980 State Prize for poetry. In it Anhava writes, often aphoristically, of the various ages of man. She is married to the poet, Tuomas Anhava.

MY SONS HAVE GROWN TO MANHOOD

Now that they have grown to the age of killers
my mind turns inside out from anguish.
Sometimes I think that the grief of mothers
has been handed down to me through the genes.
Have I told you
that my grandmother had five sons
of which two fell in the civil war
—their memory sleeps on a ridge
between two waters—
the fifteen-year old in Ahvola,
the middle one as a prisoner at Maitiaislahti,
they dug him up from a common grave, wrapped in a sheet
at the end of May,
identified by his fingers.
What had happened to his face
was never said out loud.

My sons have grown to manhood
and suddenly I see them moving through doors
at every age: creeping, crawling,
long haired, bearded,
and the mother in me still believes
that there is no cause
for which the young should die.
Everytime a son was born
I thought: I will not give him up to war,
even if I have to hide him.

AMONG THE GRIEVING
ONE SHOULD SPEAK SOFTLY

If we were a generation that was led astray
make sure that you are not,
if we were taught two colors,
why should your perception be as narrow
with only the angle of the picture changed.
You laugh and applaud in the strangest places
so that I have to perk up my ears.
Have you ever met anyone
who is overwhelmed by everlasting sorrow?
No? I can introduce a few—
a woman who got her husband back in a coffin,
"Do not open" written on the top;
another, to whom her executed husband's body
was returned after the military's psychiatric test had
     judged him sane:
fear is a crime, it creates panic.
Did you laugh, at what point did you applaud?
Would you like to conduct an interview, a small Gallup poll,
you could perhaps ask how it feels to live one's life
     from beginning to end
during a time in which you talk about the past
as though about a good joke, about those who were
     crazy about the war.
Among the grieving, one should speak softly
   about things one may have difficulty reliving.
This is not a time for applause, it is a time to listen,
not a time for trite, ready-made phrases
but to listen with sensitivity
allow one to filter each matter through one's own mind
     and heart,
also heart, since emotions are not the opposite of intellect,
they are a part of it.
You may look at the world as at a black and white diagram,
but not at life and people,
for that you need shadings and much emotion,
experienced, not taught,

"you cannot go through life the way you go through a field,"
says Pasternak.
You cannot go through life the way you go through a field.

Kun se jolta sait elämän
                on kivulla lähtenyt,
on kuin keinu pysähtyisi,
maailma humahtaisi kuulumattomiin.
Näet hiljaisen talon maisemassa,
lapset heinänkorkuisina sen edessä,
joku avaa vintin ikkunan,
pihlaja tekee marjaa.
Lähestyt sitä hitaasti
järveltä päin
ja jokainen kahahdus,
tuoksu, suhina
tepäisee väylät auki
lapsuuden kaikkiin kesiin.

CHILDHOOD SUMMERS

When she who gave you life
                    has departed with pain,
it is as though a swing halts,
the world smiles unhearing.
You see a quiet house on the landscape,
the children, tall as the grass, before it,
someone opens the attic window,
the mountain ash is full of berries.
You approach slowly
from the lakeside
and every rustle,
fragrance, murmur
opens the passages
to all childhood summers.

TUOMAS ANHAVA

TUOMAS ANHAVA
(1927-   )

A poet, essayist, critic and translator, Tuomas Anhava helped spearhead the modernist movement in Finnish poetry in the 1950s. He is well known as a guide and mentor of two generations of younger poets. Among his "finds" are Paavo Haavikko, Veijo Meri, and Pentti Saarikoski. He served as editor of *Parnasso*, leading literary journal in Finland, from 1966-1969.

Anhava has published six volumes of poetry. They reveal a classical temperament, a search for the absolute. His later poems lean toward Eastern philosophy. He has shown great interest in the poetry of Japan and China. He is a master of the short poem—epigram, haiku—with a philosophical humor that is a major element in much of his poetry. A highly intellectual man, he often attacks intellect and learning in his poems. In his later poems he appears to accept the world as it is.

His translations into Finnish include Blake's *The Marriage of Heaven and Hell, Anabase* by St. John Perse, works by T.S. Eliot, Ezra Pound and C.P. Cavafy, and a selection of *tanka* poems called *I Listen, Stranger*.

In 1976 he was awarded the prestigious Alexis Kivi Award. He has also received State Prizes for literature and translations.

He received a Master's degree from the University of Helsinki in 1947, and was appointed Professor of Arts from 1970-1975, an honorary position not affiliated with a specific university but with a secured income. He is married to the poet Helena Anhava.

128

THE SKY HAS WINGS

The sky has wings, the tin roof shines.
The maple by the yard, shadeless tree,
drops its windless leaves.
A barren vine clings
to the naked brick wall.

A moist cold wind wipes the face empty.
Birds fly briefly, of necessity.
The cemetery's multi-colored grounds slow down departure.
Hollow storms
push their noisy way through the city at night.

From year to year the world is more real.
I remember everything. Everything happens.
Everything at once,
and gloriously at once, like the autumn sun,
October brightness, or the sea's deep warmth.

MAY 1964

V

The last day of May, of the last May
tomorrow we will not see
but May leafs out toward June
in the morning a dove covered with dust turned his head
                              and awakened
the sun shone, the air was blue to breathe
the sun shines, the air is clear
and in the middle of pay day, in the middle of reckoning
I come out of the bank
and I am filled with the wonder of what is happening
filled with tenderness
women! women like perennials on the street, men like wardrobes
taking steps
the sun shines, cars howl
streetcars trucks uncomprehending armies
If it has rained, where does the fragrance from the grove go?
Why does the branch fall this way across the path?
where is the cloud going?
When no one is there, what is blue?

I go through the door,
the elevator jerks, doors slam,
the world is a city and does not stop, my rooms fill with
                              the bustle
the bustle that does not stop, oh, suddenly all is still:
                              sometimes it is.
The rooms gather that too
the window open.
Then something clangs. A boy whistles. Downstairs in the yard.
No melody. Just whistling.

I SLEEP TO THE PATTER OF THE RAIN

I sleep to the patter of the rain, to the jabber of my child,
I sleep to long stories that I read to my sons who were
                    impatient with the rain,
My breathing steadies and I am as though I were not,
in me awakens the rainy day's entire long memory,
I remember the rock where I lay filled with awareness and pain.
My son came and he had worries
and I said something silly,
and he laughed straight through his tears
and his tears moved to me, who understands.

Nukun sateen sokellukseen, lapsen jokellukseen,
minä nukun pitkiin tarinoihin joita luen pojille
                    sateesta kärsimättömille,
hengitykseni tasaantuu ja minä olen kuin en,
minussa havahtuu sateisen päivän koko pitkä muisti,
muistan kallion jolla makasin täynnä tajua ja kipua.
Poikani tuli ja hänellä oli huolta
ja minä sanoin jotain hullunkurista,
ja hän nauroi suoraan itkun lävitse
ja itku siirtyi minuun, joka tiedän.

EEVA KILPI

EEVA KILPI
(1928-   )

In 1972, when the peak of politically oriented literature in Finland was past, Eeva Kilpi wrote in a poem, "You may believe that everything is political,/I believe that every day is a story," and thus showed the direction of the new literature.

Kilpi was then well established as a respected novelist and writer of short stories. As a "new voice" in poetry, she has published three enthusiastically received collections in the last ten years: *Laulu rakkaudesta* (Song of Love, 1972), *Terveisin* (Greetings, 1976), and *Ennen kuolemaa* (Before Death, 1982). In *Ennen kuolemaa* she takes the reader with her day by day through her pain, through the gradual changes in the grieving process after the death of her beloved father. It is a profound experience.

Kilpi's poetry is intimate, disarmingly honest, deeply perceptive— sensitive, reflective poems couched in the tone of everyday speech. Her respect for nature is beautifully revealed, and her delightfully sharp wit adds zest to her writing.

Kilpi grew up in Karelia, an area of southeastern Finland ceded to the Russians after the Winter War, 1939-40. Then a girl of eleven, she and her family and hundreds of thousands of other Karelians had to leave their homes forever.

Kilpi received a Master's degree from the University of Helsinki in 1953. She was awarded State Prizes for literature in 1967 and 1973. She served as chairman of the Finnish P.E.N. Club from 1970-1975.

HE STEPPED INSIDE MY DOOR

Let me know right away if I'm disturbing you,
he said as he stepped inside my door,
and I'll leave the way I came.

Not only do you disturb me,
I answered,
you turn my whole world upside down.
Welcome.

AND DREAMS PALED

No sooner had I learned to get along without
than I happened to think:
I will not give up this person.

And the sheets burst into bloom.
This is reality, he said,
and dreams paled.

So that was the kind of force
behind those civilized glances
that for years
we gave each other.

* * *

Even nature gives you no choice.

When you have seen a cloud in the lap of a pond
and the moon between the waterlilies,
inevitably you are at the mercy of your own soul.

* * *

—What is this sound that wakens me at night?

—It is biology, it calls out its rights.
At night you can hear it more clearly
when the sociologists are sleeping

* * *

THE FIFTH DAY

A heavy feeling.
Fifth day since the funeral.
The everyday life of grief has begun;
Mother already looks like a widow.
Father should come to comfort us.

But he won't come.
Evening will come and morning will come
and the sixth day.

WHERE BEHIND THE NIGHT DID YOU GET LOST

Every morning Father is dead
always just dead
every day dead
every evening

where behind the night did you get lost, my golden swan
in what lands, foreign

snow falls
and sleet
and rain

cold is coming
snowdrifts
and ice

chopped ice and a chilling hole in the ice
a blizzard and a long journey

hurry home
cancel your flight

we are here
without a father, orphans
your wife, an orphan
daughters, orphans
family, orphaned
kin orphaned
I the most orphaned of orphans
evening comes, night
not Father.

ONE MORNING THE EARTH STIRRED

One morning the earth stirred and shook the people from its shoulders like vermin; also earth's do-gooders. They spattered out into space like lice or stars. Some self-important politicians it killed with its claw, some bourgeois it kicked in the pants and some brawling radicals it blew into the air like feathers. And when it had been freed at last from these hornets, it sighed deeply, settled down to rest and began to flower from every crack.

WEATHER FORECASTERS

Of those the gods hate more than teachers
they make weather forecasters.
Each time the wind turns
they feel it in their bones.
When rain is on the way
they are at death's door.
Cold's vultures peck at their shoulders,
dig at their necks,
sit on their knees,
tear at their toes,
feast on their tendons and connective tissue.
Pains dart from their loins to their calves,
bite there, strike here,
swell and multiply
before low pressure sets in.
They rest seldom, in the sun.
And as if that isn't enough,
the gods make them long-lived.

THISTLE

Thistle, autumn's last to flower.
Restrained, pale bluish-red.
Strong stem, won't fall in the rain,
won't bend in the wind.
Prickly: natural selection.

On top a nettle-butterfly.
Large, new, just emerged,
freshly colored,
in its last stage of life:
as a butterfly, at its best.

And all this multiplied:
dense, misty area
firm and fluttery—before its death
summer gave birth to this phenomenon
to say farewell to creation.

Small shrikes, late to migrate,
perch on the roof's edge
feasting on butterflies
fed by the field of thistles.
Painful to be an observer
of nature's balance and harmony.

But what would be better?
Be a scarecrow.
Pull out the thistles.
Start a cabbage patch?

Autumn knows:
the shrikes are leaving,
the butterflies linger,
scent of thistles fills the air,
sweetness runs wild.
It is beautiful to die.

A MIDSUMMER'S ROSE

This morning I have decided not to write
but to plant a rose.

So this is what a person needs in order to be happy:
work, that one may put it aside,
sensitivity, that one may feel that it is justified,
and a childhood
that one may have roots for a midsummer's rose
to climb on the wall of one's old age.

Tänä aamuna olen päättänyt olla kirjoittamatta
ja istuttaa ruusun.

Siis tätä ihminen tarvitsee ollakseen onnellinen:
työn että voi lyödä sen laimin,
helteen että tuntee sen oikeutetuksi
ja lapsuuden
että voi juuria siitä juhannusruusun
vanhuutensa seinustalle.

TOMORROW I WILL HEAT THE SAUNA

As I go to bed, I think:
Tomorrow I will heat the sauna,
be good to myself,
take me for a walk, swim, bathe,
invite myself for evening tea,
speak to myself with kindness
    and admiration,
offer praise: you small brave woman,
I trust you.

VEIJO MERI

VEIJO MERI
(1928-   )

Veijo Meri is generally regarded as the leader of Finnish modernist prose. In recent years he has also published three collections of poetry. He is an exponent of the anti-hero and a shrewd and humorous commentator on family life. His humor is often grim and dry. Translations of his prose works have appeared in sixteen languages. Among his poetry collections are *Mielen Lähtolaskenta* (Mental countdown, 1976) and *Toinen sydän* (Another Heart, 1978). His numerous literary awards include six State Prizes for literature and the prestigious Nordic Council Literature Prize in 1974.

A graduate of the University of Helsinki (1948), he was appointed Professor of Arts in 1974, an honorary title which carries a substantial stipend for a period of years.

RHYTHM

Pitch and quantity struggle in our words
and rock them back and forth constantly.
I flop flat on my stomach on top of them
so they won't rise up
like any glued corners that have come loose.
One continual rocking
this language just like this life.
When you lie on top of it, it starts
to throb like a cushioned woman's heart.

Once we breathed together to the same beat
for two minutes, until we noticed
it. You had a bottle of red wine,
I a schnaps glass of cactus liquor.
Is that what gave us the same rhythm?
Are we so much different?

Pyöreä on maailma,
pyöreä kuin aurinko.
Kello on sen kuva.
Viisarit, varjojen liike,
varjot, orjuutettu yö,
palvelijoiksi pestattu kansa.
Itseään silpoo kuu,
pilkkaa tätä kaikkea.
Kesä lopulla, syksyllä
kuu on täysi, pyöreä,
kaupunki on sen metsä,
rivi talvitauluja.
Kuoleman ote ei pidä,
kaikki kuollut katoaa.
Monta miljoonaa
maailmaa täynnä elämää
kuoli ennen meitä.
Mikä ihmeellinen onni
elää täällä juuri nyt.

THE WORLD IS ROUND

The world is round,
round like the sun.
The clock is its image.
Hands of the clock, movement of shadows,
shadows, enslaved night,
nation recruited into servitude.
The moon mutilates itself,
ridicules it all.
At summer's end, in the fall
the moon is full, round,
city is its forest,
row of winter landscapes.
Death's grip doesn't hold,
all that is dead disappears.
Many million
worlds filled with life
died before us.
What wonderful fortune
to live here right now.

BUCHAREST

We drank red wine in Bucharest.
We saw blue-eyed Turks,
absoluteness of truth,
our ability to evade it,
the superior tactics
with which we avoid responsibility.
Puzzled, we looked at those who
felt they had the right
to claim that their integrity
was greater than our forthrightness.
This is an example of that.

A lovely young woman's despair
at the embassy door
because of her only son's death.
She came to get spiritual support
from the ambassador's office.

We gave her the easiest advice.
Travel to Finland, travel.
Week-old torn and crumpled newspapers
translated into miserable German.
We returned pencils, bowed.
Outside we encountered the stare of the militia
and an equally clean and perfect uniform
and the dirtiest of all, November.

WHEN I WAS YOUNG

When I was young
I had all of this
and an endless amount of time
to go past this.
I even had a family:
children, father and mother.
Only now my position is different,
experienced how it feels to wear
a father's pants, take them off.

PERTTI NIEMINEN

PERTTI NIEMINEN
(1929-   )

Pertti Nieminen is a modern classic poet, a man of humor and deep sensitivity. In his seventh collection, *Huomisella on vielä omat huolensa* (Tomorrow Brings Its Own Worries, 1979), he writes with a gentle and sometimes painful irony about modern people, especially himself. In 1981 he published a book of poems about his grandchildren, *Kuusi silmää, kuusi korvaa* (Six Eyes, Six Ears).

Known as an exceptionally gifted translator of Chinese poetry, Nieminen views the present through the mirror of Oriental antiquity, the changelessness of change, and the endless repetition of history. His translations include *Tao-te-king*, an anthology of *Chinese Storytellers*, and *The Great Wind, Jade Wood, Autumn Voice*.

Nieminen received a University degree in 1948 and was an instructor of Chinese Literature at the University of Helsinki from 1972-1976. He was awarded a State Prize for poetry in 1964 and for translations in 1970.

154

THAT'S NOT A TIGER

You are mistaken: that's not a tiger, black as night, that roars—
the mountains are rumbling from the force of the wind
and leaves of the aspen are rattling under the rain.
Don't be afraid: I'll turn on the yard light and lend you
                    an umbrella.
Today the army troops are marching far from here,
                    far from here they are attacking:
go in peace, there are no bodies on the road,
spirits in the forest, a bat or two circles around the light,
at the gate a shadow sways.

Now cook some soup from mushrooms,
make tea and fetch a bottle from the cellar:
the guests have left, it is time to eat and drink.
The window can stay open a little, we will air out the fear
and the aroma of tea is even better when the air is fresh.
When the flower of the wine has opened, I will say:
the touch of silk against me is like the touch of your skin;
the guests are already home, they won't turn back—
come, let's go to sleep,
let's sleep in each others arms.

MY SISTER

My sister was born when I was three and a half.
I can't imagine how she would look now,
when my hair is beginning to gray.
I only remember a boisterous companion,
so contrary, so cross or tender,
and I especially remember
she feared nothing,
not lizards or spiders,
not bombers or the dark.

My sister died in the last years of the war,
in my arms.
That is when I realized my love for her
and longing, which does not end.

I DRINK THE WINE OF YOUR DREAMS

My sons' dreams smell of clay and grass,
of camp fires and bulrushes, of hot iron, of clouds,
my daughters' dreams come from the wind of the field,
from flowers of the willow, clouds;
in your dreams is the fragrance of the almond tree,
the fragrance of unlit Havana cigars and shores of Bahi,
of unknown wine and unknown waters,
fragrance of aspen groves and Turkestan;
when you sleep the room grows with wild apple trees,
the meadow rocks and a stream opens
and sandalwood burns;
when you are asleep I come,
I swim in the rivers of your dreams, drink the wine
                    of your dreams,
hide in the forests of your dreams and coax you to come with me
ever deeper.

Kun lähestyin viittäkymmentä,
aloin taas kuulla sirkkojen laulun.
Kesäkuussa ei ilta pimene, yö vain hämärtyy,
ja hämärissä laulavat isot sirkat,
kirkonkokoiset.
Kuvitelkaa hämmästystäni,
kun avasin ikkunan ja kuulin sirityksen:
se täytti maailman, taukoamattaan.
Puut ja oraat lauloivat nuorta kesää
suoraan vanhoihin korviini,
    joiden ei pitäisi enää kuulla.

WHEN I NEARED FIFTY*

When I neared fifty,
I began again to hear crickets singing.
In June, evening doesn't darken,
                    only night dims,
and in the dusk large crickets sing,
big as churches.
Imagine my surprise,
when I opened the window and heard a chirping:
it filled the world, without pausing.
Trees and sprouts sang the young summer
into my ears,
            too old to hear.

In Finnish folklore, one indication of growing old is when one can no longer hear
the crickets sing.

THEY WERE PURE GOLD

Father, erect and wise,
humble only before nature;
Mother, proud of being a woman,
to us gentle and loving.
Perhaps I still don't know, you say,
where the *puna-ailakit* grow,
nor can I feel in my hand
      the trunk of the cherry tree
that froze during the winter war; nor do I remember
the call of the woodpecker in the middle of the city
before rain. Little by little
I have begun to understand
that it's not time that makes those memories golden;
they were pure gold
when they evolved. But how many
might I have thrown away?
Actually thrown away.

PAAVO HAAVIKKO

PAAVO HAAVIKKO
(1931-   )

Paavo Haavikko is the acknowledged great master of the Fifties modernist movement in Finnish poetry. He is credited with freeing the language of the poets from the Kalevala tradition and leading it toward a very personal form of ironical existentialism. Haavikko's own poetry depends on paradox, irony, legends, and on conservative political ideology. He is extremely interested in understanding history, including the Kalevala tradition. Some of his poems are about well-defined historical events, such as "A Finnish Suite" in *Lehdet lehtiä* (Leaves the Leaves, 1958), which deals with Russia's annexation of Finland in 1809. Most of Haavikko's work, however, is truly transnational in concept. He has stated that his main themes are metaphysics, death and love. His poetry has been compared with that of Wallace Stevens.

Haavikko's nine-poem cycle *Talvipalasti* (Winter Palace, 1959) is one of the landmarks of modern Finnish literature. He calls it "a journey through the known language," a poem about poetry. It has been compared with *The Waste Land.* One of Haavikko's latest collections of poetry is *Viiniä, kirjoitusta* (Wine, Writings, 1976).

Haavikko is also a novelist and a playwright. He has served as an executive of the Otava publishing house in Helsinki for several years. He has a degree from the University of Helsinki, 1951. Haavikko has been the recipient of numerous State Prizes for poetry and literature since 1958.

162

WHEN I NOW TELL YOU ABOUT THE EMPEROR

When I now tell you about the Emperor you see him,
the Emperor, all of a sudden,
when I now tell you about the Emperor you see:
it is winter, the Emperor is alone,
the Emperor is an image that becomes clearer in the dusk,
the Emperor is an image,
dusk is coming,
there is a tangle of trees like an eagle's nest on a slope,
the dry thickness of branches,
and the Emperor is alone and his image is clear,
he is at his summer retreat which is cold in winter,
he is the one you see most clearly in the dark,
and thought, bird, owl, your unseeing thought
can also still see the Emperor in the dark.

I have led you astray and you stand beside a wintry mountain
and you try to look through the branches at the Emperor
that is not,

when you close your eyes you again see him
in his summer retreat
and his image is clear,

I have led you astray, open your eyes and don't listen to me,

the strength of the Empire is in your heart, there it is strong,
the Empire rises and falls with the blinking of an eye,

it dies when the eyes open.

Elämän kirjurit, kirjoittakaa
kultaiseen kirjaan.

Minä olen maailman iltalaulu, sitra,
unen punaisen marmorin veistäjä
olen, maailman ovenpielet palavat,
pikisoihdut, savuten,
kasvoni, Neron kasvot ovat naamio,
jos punainen,
niin verta itkee metsä pohjoisessa,
tulta ratsut pärskyvät maailmaa päin,
jos punainen, tyhjä,
pääkallonaamio, sulaa lyijyä juonut silmin
ja kääntyneenä pois kuin sureva nainen,
on maailma mennyttä,
puhkaistu pimeydet, oi pimeydet,
minä hymyilen,
maailman kantajien kasvot halkeavat hymyyn,
jumalan, keisarin, näyttelijän, Neron kasvot
kääntyvät pois, menen pois Oinotriasta,
varjot ilveilevät.

RECORDERS OF LIFE

Recorders of life, write
in your golden book.

I am the world's evening song, zither,
sculptor of sleep's red marble
I am, the world's doorposts burn,
torches, smoking,
my face, Nero's face is a mask,
if red,
then a forest in the north cries blood,
horses spatter fire toward the world,
if red, empty,
skull mask, melted lead consumed by its eyes
and turned away like a sorrowing woman,
world is gone,
pierced darknesses, oh darknesses,
I smile,
faces of the world's pallbearers break into smiles,
god's, emperor's, actor's, Nero's face
turn away, I leave Oinotria,*
shadows mock.

*The Greek name for the toe of the foot of Italy where the Trojans landed.

I LOOK OUTSIDE

I look outside, fireplace flames in the window, burn
    against rain, smoke, green alders.
I reflect how my world is already behind so many wars:
the door opening behind me is the frame where you see me
    coming,
        going, before I turn and go,
and that the house, house, love and joyous times
    don't always chance to coincide.

Katson ulos, uunin tuli on ikkunalasissa, palaa
    sadetta, savua, vihreitä leppiä vasten.
Mietin, miten monen sodan takana on jo maailmani;
oviaukko takana on se kehys jossa sinä näet minut
    tulossa,
        menossa, ennen kuin käännyn ja menen,
ja että talo, talo, rakkaus ja iloiset ajat
    eivät aina niin vain satu yhteen.

MIRKKA REKOLA

MIRKKA REKOLA
(1931-   )

Mirkka Rekola, who began publishing poetry in 1954, joined poets of the first rank who were breathing new strength into Finnish poetry with her collections *Ilo ja epäsymmetria* (Joy and Symmetry, 1965) and *Anna päivän olla kaikki* (Let the Day Be All, 1968). Her concentrated language has continued to extend the expressive range of Finnish. Rekola is a master of the "silent poem." Her powerful introspection is a breath-taking experience. Fundamentally she is a mystic.

Rekola was awarded the prestigious Eino Leino Prize for poetry in 1979 and earlier was awarded three State Prizes for poetry. She has a degree from the University of Helsinki (1954).

Recently Rekola has revived, with two collections of aphorisms, this genre of Finnish literature. Her most recent books include her ninth collection of poetry, *Kohtaamispaikka vuosi* (Meeting Place of the Year, 1977) and *Kuutamourakka* (Moonlighting, 1981).

168

AMONG DARK TREES

On top of this long hill
I got you to sit on the sled,
there were no longer children on the hill, it was so late,
you sat down, I gave a push,
watched as it went,
$\qquad\qquad$ your back,
how it narrowed, narrowed, there
among dark trees you were in your childhood.

Tämän pitkän mäen päällä
minä sain sinut istumaan pulkkaan,
ei ollut enää lapsiakaan mäessä,
$\qquad\qquad$ oli niin myöhä,
siinä istuit, minä annoin vauhtia,
katselin kun se meni,
$\qquad\qquad$ sinun selkäsi,
kuinka se kapeni, kapeni, tuolla tummien
puiden lomassa sinä olit lapsuudessa.

IN THIS WIND

I should speak
as though in my words
there still were sound
and you would answer everything near you
in this wind
that comes in the beginning
goes over and around incessantly
                          here we are
the same age
we could call out together

YOU REMEMBER THE ELK

You remember the elk that took
the direction of the sun
and even so it darkened,
you remember death in a yellow tree,
the lamp's heart,
and this is only a yawn and a rock protruding
toward a big region.

VÄINÖ KIRSTINÄ

VÄINÖ KIRSTINÄ
(1936-   )

A Post-modernist poet, Väinö Kirstinä was known in the 'sixties as an experimenter, teacher, theorist, and a translator of note. His poetry was a major source of inspiration to young poets of that period. His poetry continues to bear the mark of his individual, refreshing personality. Among his works are *Puhetta* (Talk, 1963), *Luonnollinen tanssi* (A Natural Dance, 1965), and *Talo Maalla* (House in the Country, 1969). A collection of his poems (1958-1977) was published in 1979. In 1963 he was awarded the State Prize for poetry. Kirstinä has translated Baudelaire's *Le Spleen de Paris,* and some of his own poems are reminiscent in form and content of Jacques Prévert's work.

Kirstinä received a Master's degree from the University of Helsinki in 1963. He has worked as a newspaper reporter and as a Finnish language instructor.

YOU WILL SEE FAR

If you arrive in the land of the wind, the
                    bottom of the sea
there are few trees, a strong cold wind
from shore to shore.

You can see far
without seeing anything.

Ruskeanvihreä sammal on kasvanut harmaansinervän
kiven kylkeen. Kiven kyljessä Cesar Borgian kasvot,
turpeat Orson Wellesin kasvot.

Muissakin kivissä on hahmoja: yksi on ahven tai mur-
meli, riippuu siitä miten katsoo, toinen kivi on virta-
hevon pää, joka haukkaa ikuisesti suurta möhkalettä. Se
ei ole vieläkään nielaissut suupalaansa.

Entä jos viljelisi kivistä maata: tuottaisi sipuleita,
neilikoita, mansikoita tai villaa? Virkamieheksi en sovi;
maanviljelijän ammatti on minun sukuni perinne, ja minä
olen satunnainen poikkeus, seikkailija ellen huijari.

THIS ROCKY LAND

Brownish green moss has grown into the side of gray blue
rock. On the side of the rock the face of Cesare Borgia,
the bloated face of Orson Welles.

There are shapes on other rocks too: one is a perch or a
marmot, depends on how you look at it, another rock is
the head of a hippopotamus that eternally bites of a big
chunk. It still hasn't swallowed one mouthful.

What if I were to cultivate this rocky land: perhaps
grow onions, carnations, strawberries or wool? Public
service is not for me; farming is my family's tradition,
and I am the chance exception, an adventurer if not a
charlatan.

PROPAGANDA ART

A hungry man looks into the restaurant
and watches how a glutton eats:
a small daydream, picture, poem,
propaganda art,
bad taste from the year 1957,
excellent in 1965,
and again bad three years later;
and the man continues to stand there,
and the mercury slides down with the cold
and not the reverse
like on the other side
where a small daydream is born,
picture, poem, propaganda art,
where feelings are proclaimed.

FIERCE OLD TREES

fierce old trees
      prophesy
the house in the arms of the wind

the house, mother,
the house, nest,
the house, me,

the house where we spend the night
from where we see the sunrise

which reaches toward the sky in the rain
which is rooted to the earth

and windows
and a darkening mirror on the wall

PENTTI SAARIKOSKI

PENTTI SAARIKOSKI
(1937-   )

Pentti Saarikoski is a major poet of postwar Finland. For a time he adopted the role of the Renaissance poet, a public figure selling not only his poems but his personality, and his reputation as a literary *enfant terrible* made him a symbol of unconventionality. He has, however, earned an important place in Finnish literary history for his contributions to the development of poetic methods. Viewed against a larger European context, he is an original with a strong sense of poetic traditions. His central theme is the isolated individual who wants to communicate but is crippled by ideologies that have outlived themselves.

The turning point in his writing career came in 1962 with the publication of his fifth poetry collection, *Mitä tapahtuu todella* (What is Really Going On). He abandoned the polished poetry of the 'fifties and changed to an open, conversational style, using remarks heard on the street and, above all, open political viewpoints.

Saarikoski has published fifteen volumes of poetry and five prose works. He has received the State Prize for poetry and translations several times. Among his recent poetry collections are: *Tanssilattia vuorella* (Dance Floor on the Mountain, 1977) and *Tanssiinkutsu* (Invitation to the Dance, 1980)—both based on the mythical past as well as the present.

Educated in the classics (University of Helsinki) and a brilliant translator, he has translated into Finnish Homer's *Odyssey* and writings of Aristotle, Euripides and Sappho; also the works of J.D. Salinger, Henry Miller and James Joyce's *Ulysses*. His own poetry has been translated into several languages. In 1980 Anselm Hollo, Finnish poet now living in the United States, was awarded the First Prize for poetry in English translation by the *Scandinavian Review* (published in New York), his entry being poems by Saarikoski.

For the past few years Saarikoski has lived in Sweden in self-imposed spiritual and intellectual exile.

A LONG JOURNEY

Flowery wallpaper: on the window pane painted castle and sunset.
Milkweed and wild carnations bloom on the edge of a gravel pit,
fish splash in the shallow bay
I wrote
poems, I was fourteen, the island's highest rock
was my forum,
below in the field walked a farmer.
My heart is full, I remember everything
during the war in the spring I pulled pine cones from the ice
under the pine trees,
because I could earn points for it.
Familiar wallpaper, familiar castle and sunset,
I am in a familiar place,
on a long journey from perfect order
to complete confusion.

Minä asun Helsingissä.
Helsinki on Suomen pääkaupunki.
Se sijaitsee meren rannalla 120 mailia Leningradista länteen.
Helsinki on kasvava kaupunki, ja vuokrat ovat korkeat.
Me istumme täällä metsiemme keskellä selin jättiläiseen
  ja katsomme hänen kuvaansa lähteestä. Hänella on tumma puku,
  valkoinen paita
ja
  hopeanharmaa solmio. Hänen maassaan kaikki on toisin
  kuin täällä, siellä kävellään päällään tai ilman päätä.
Me istumme omien metsien keskellä,
mutta kaukana lännessä on maa jonka rantavesissä kelluu
  isoja silmiä, ja ne näkevät tänne.
Helsinki rakennetaan uudelleen Alvar Aallon suunitelman mukaan.

I LIVE IN HELSINKI

I live in Helsinki.
Helsinki is the capitol of Finland.
It is situated by the sea 120 miles west of Leningrad.
Helsinki is a growing city, and the rents are high.
We sit here in the midst of our forests our backs to the giant
    and look at his image in a spring. He wears a dark suit,
    white shirt
and
    a silver gray tie. In this country everything is different
    from here, there people walk on their heads or without heads.
We sit in the midst of our own forests,
but far away in the west is a country in whose eastern waters
    float huge eyes, and they see us.
Helsinki is being rebuilt by Alvar Aalto's design.

PARLIAMENT HAD BEEN DISSOLVED

Parliament had been dissolved
morning newspapers would have pictures
of President Kekkonen
his face reflecting concern
Finland appears on a map
as a darker spot
like a pierced eye

I listened to the radio and thought
of a morning one summer
I walked through a park
it was quite early
on my way home
been awake all night
I looked at shrubs and the sun rose
I created poetry
little green cannons guarded the sunrise
there was no one yet on the streets
about the Berlin situation
these verbs are taken out of usage
to be used only by the Right
there is water in their trenches

what is really going on?
the air was warm that morning
as though one were in a large room looking out

A GOOD SOCIETY

A good society is one
   where people don't even think of
presenting demands that the society
   cannot fulfill

the window sill curves over the radiator
   books gather dust
   there is a bomb in the refrigerator
   pine branches sway

   I'm beginning to feel sorry for
   Tanner and Leskinen
   Tanner now such an old man
   and Leskinen still so young

the overthrow of the lawful society order
   is an unlawful act
   even if the whole world were to change
   Finland will preserve its traditions
   banana peels darken in the corner
who could find better windows for Khrushchev

   when there is light inside a bird it flies
   above the forest
   an old wives' tale
on the floor a twisted metallic letter of the alphabet

THE SUN SETS, SUN RISES

Lofty poetry, the sun sets, sun rises
Sun burns
the cannons are hollow arms without hands
into which it rains

a bird that dives tail first
                    and calls KTO KOVO KTO KVO

is a Weapon

            the forest divides there is a road
there is Khrushchev
                            no road
            What is Europe
        the frog jumps its nose under a rock

and:
a church full of women a bull bellows a hundred bulls,
a Negro sheds his skin,
a Republican and a Democrat embrace for the last time,
the one crucified turns in the wind nor will the world
                            be saved unless it turns,
America directs Europe by its hind legs and Castro is
                            the Statue of Liberty
and:

ideological contents: shadows of deeds that embrace
the one crucified jingles like a growing city
over a child a lovely castle

HISTORY OF THE REVOLUTION

In his well-known History of the Revolution, Trotsky tells
        when Lenin
        had eyeglasses and a toupee
                and it rained in St. Petersburg
                Mother Russia gave birth to a child
        who was to become . . .

when the serving had stopped
        customers have been hurried out
        chairs stacked on top of tables
                and the cashier is counting the monty
        when you look at this from the outside
        and everything is as usual
                and continues and has continued . . .

the car looks like a million I am sheer
                darkness like an angel
        who flies faster than its own light

On two tables I spread out old legends
shields and spears and fire
shoulders thrusting forward
man against man in war
armor rattling
each hurled into dust
and death's night approaches
In the morning we talked about the war
the one now being waged
the nature of which gradually reveals itself
this is not the kind in which men fall
or where there is a shortage of soap
When we see what is happening to us
we know what they want from us
but not who they are

When I walk to the seashore
birds fly from a tree
suddenly as though shedding its leaves
and I shiver
I simplify the world
into a labyrinth

in whose heart pants a Minotaur
born from forbidden love
a machine
its propelling power living cells
and its purpose
to develop the labyrinth into an ever better shelter

Only when the Minotaur is destroyed
and the labyrinth has become a dance
are *politeia* and politics again possible
That is the nature of this war

It is not difficult to find the Minotaur
more difficult to destroy it
most difficult to find one's way out of the labyrinth

When I walk to the seashore, I say again and again
the brightest, the purest
Aridela! Arihagne!
Nether world purity! Heavenly brightness!
We need so much faith
no one has the strength
to carry it alone
old legends
on two tables,
I walk
to the seashore
waiting
for so many years now that every sail
would appear black in my eyes

from *Dance Floor on the Mountain*

191

XXX

Tyrants were
people
who undressed
and dressed
worked late into the night
moved papers
and citizens
from incoming mail
to outgoing mail
now the heart is gone
from government
tyrants rationalized away
machines that
don't tire
don't drink themselves into oblivion
don't do a Cossack dance
do their work
they speak as though pulling barbed wire
and you hear
what you are
you are number one two three
or four five six seven
or zero
these machines wouldn't be possible
had they not been invented

from *Invitation to a Dance*

SIRKKA TURKKA

SIRKKA TURKKA
(1939-   )

Sirkka Turkka emerged as a significant Finnish poet in the early 'seventies. To date she has published five collections of poetry and one work of prose. Her poetry includes *Mies joka rakasti vaimoaan liikaa* (The Man Who Loved His Wife Too Much, 1979) and *Kaunis hallitsija* (Beautiful Sovereign, 1981). In much of her work the theme of death is close at hand. "I speak of death when I mean to speak of life," she writes in one of her poems.

Turkka is a story teller, a ballad singer, a reciter of epic tales. She is an innate master of language, a lyricist whose voice is perceptive and persuasive. Her poetry is remindful of this century's Latin-American writers, or the music of Heitor Villa-Lobos.

Turkka has a degree in humanities from the University of Helsinki (1967), and she passed a stablemaster's examination in 1970. She is employed as a stablemaster at the Espoo stables near Helsinki.

POEMS OF PAIN

Poems of pain in a year of pain.
Sorrow so full and broken
like a tired swan or scythe
by the pier, at the food of the mail box.
The Sovereign goes away,
inside the earth, which he loves.
He is Johnny Be Good,
he is a maiden in the water,
on all the flags is a picture of a furry dog.
At night you can't return to the hotel
from the other side of the river.
The lift bridges are up.
Flags at half mast.
Until earth is earth,
until heart's silt blends.
Listen, Sovereign:
eternally this eternal flame.
Violets burning above the flame
and people drinking water
at the root of funeral music.

Näin puiden putoavan.
Rakkaus kimmeltää pienenä saarena
keskellä silmää, minun rakkauteni,
joka on metsä.
Ja aikaa on loputtomasti, nuku,
levähdä vielä korvahuvilassa,
sillä aikaa ei ole.
On veden liike maan yli
ja sinun elämäsi liike sinun
itsesi yli.
Ja metsät.
Ja puun toive
mennä metsään,
täyttyä ja kadota
ikuisesti.
Kuin aika jota ei ollut,
jota ei koskaan ole.

I SEE TREES FALLING

I see trees falling.
Love glistens, a small island
in the center of the eye, my love,
which is a forest.
And time is endless, sleep,
rest a while in your retreat,
since time does not exist.
There is movement of water over the earth
and movement of your life
over you.
And forests.
And the hope of a tree
to enter the forest,
to be fulfilled and disappear
forever.
Like time that never was,
that never will be.

THUS THE TREES CHANGE PLACES

Thus the trees change places, thus
they dance in step.
Notre Dame. Oh, Merciful.
Pious praise rises in smoky clusters
on your doorpost.
The sky does not split firewood on a person's back today,
only clear squares of moss disappear into the forest,
silent, the low grass listens.
Oh, Merciful, take away the sins from our backs, that which
weigh us down like bread.
That which is put in our hand every single day.
The road's clay slides and sings,
bread sings over our heads
heavy with rain and far down.
There was so much love, so little hope.
There was so much love and little hope
and tormented grayness. And weight.
Not of mountains or of rocks, only of water, of tears,
only of sorrow that eats us.

TENDERNESS CLOSED LIKE A FLOWER

There is no mercy anywhere.
Tenderness closed like a flower.
Mercy. That life had
none to give.
Only one solitary jackdaw
flies here and there, below it
wander small horses, poor things, from whom
emptiness rises with a rumble.
Dust covers the yard, there is only our
dusty field and farther
Donner's blue field.
The yard empty as the edge of a glass
and jackdaws, birds of sorrow
they are, hard as stones,
when they fly that way
against the wind.
The suffering shadows of the small horses
continually wind around the same circle.
There is no mercy.
There is the dust that covers everything.
And then the snow that covers
the flower's home in the snow.

WHEN THE SOVEREIGN ASKS

The Black Sea really was extremely black.
Would you care for a cigaret.
When the Soveriegn asks, you answer
and smoke that cigaret.
Or off with your head.
What is a champagne swan,
what a heavenly ballet.
What is green and stands in a field.
If you don't answer: a raw horse,
then it's off again with your head.

YOU ARE BORN AGAIN AND AGAIN

Since it cannot be avoided
you turn the whole time,
you are born from rain, kisses,
are mixed together and are born
again and again like a mirror.
When all the words
have been said,
life strikes.
And you are not
its master, it is not of death.
It gouges out your eyes,
it breaks your heart.
Its edge bites
ever deeper:
such a small storm took you,
I will not make you ever again.

PENTTI SAARITSA

PENTTI SAARITSA
(1941-   )

Pentti Saaritsa is one of Finland's leading left-wing poets. He writes about a wide range of social and individual themes. Among his nine collections of poetry are: *Tritonus* (Tritone, 1973), *Nautinnon Suola* (Salt of Pleasure, 1978), and *Yhdeksäs aalto* (The Ninth Wave, 1977). Both his poetry and his translations have received several State Prizes for Literature in the past fifteen years. An outstanding translator, he has translated the works of Latin American writers Pablo Neruda and Miguel Angel Asturias, as well as the works of some Russian writers. His own poetry has been translated into Swedish, French and English.

Saaritsa has a degree from the University of Helsinki, where he was the cultural editor of the University newspaper. For several years he served as a member of the editorial board of the literary quarterly, *Books from Finland*. He was also editor of the newspaper of Finland's Social Democratic Party.

SALT OF PLEASURE

Vacuous childhood,
window fogged by sprinkles
and milkwhite stillness,
awaiting.
There *is* no emptiness.
Look at it, stare
until it begins to live.
In emptiness throb the arteries
of a kingdom, potential.
And from what you lack
you gather yourself.
The rain rinses the window clear, the sun
dries the tears, and look,
your landscape lives and must be witnessed.
On your cheeks, the salt of pleasure.

Virikkeetön lapsuus,
pisaroiden sumentama ikkuna
ja maidonvalkea hiljaisuus,
odotava.
Ei ole tyhjyyttä.
Katso siihen, tuijota
kunnes se alkaa elää.
Sillä tyhjyydessä värähtelee suonistona
valtakunta, potentia.
Ja siitä mikä sinulta puuttuu
sinä kokoat itsesi.
Sade huuhtoo ikkunan kirkkaaksi, aurinko
kuivaa kyynelet, ja katso,
sinun maisemasi elää ja on todistettava.
Poskillasi nautinnon suola.

WE WERE SUNTANNED GODS

I walked past you.
You walked through me.
We were suntanned gods,
immortal beasts.

Something branded us.
It struck a deep wound in my forehead
and with two big thumbs
it pushed my eyes deeper.
It carved a dark exclamation point
                              across your stomach
and your breasts dropped slightly.

It was not you, it was not I
who branded us.
It was the life
we dared to live.

VOICE OF MY BROTHERS

In the middle of noisy children
                        and general commotion
I concentrate and press my head
against the side of a mountain, against that
which we know about ourselves
and try to hear
the voice of my brothers.
I know from where it is carried, I would hear it
had I only patience to wait.

On this slope I am naked against the wind
and the cold sheets of clouds.

HANNU MÄKELÄ

HANNU MÄKELÄ
(1943-   )

Hannu Mäkelä, one of the most versatile and prolific younger writers of Finland, was awarded the esteemed Eino Leino Prize for poetry in 1982. He is also known for his children's stories, particularly his books about "Mr. Huu," which have attracted attention outside of Finland and have been translated into Swedish, Hungarian, and Polish. He was awarded State Prizes for children's stories in 1973 and 1975 and for poetry in 1981. He is also a novelist and a playwright for radio and theater.

Mäkelä has published nine volumes of poetry. His most recent are *Illan varjo* (Evening Shadow, 1979) and *Ikään kuin ihminen* (Just Like a Human, 1980). In *Illan varjo* he examines with quiet sensitity human relations seen both inwardly and outwardly. In his latest work, he continues in his seemingly peaceful, but in reality intense way, to write of loneliness, childhood, restlessness—the sorrows and challenges of modern life.

A graduate of the University of Helsinki (1962), Mäkelä now heads the Department of Literature at Otava, a major publishing house in Helsinki. He has edited two collections of Eino Leino's poetry.

GARDEN

Garden, made by man.
Soil attended by many hands.
Living earth that must be fed.
Worm, blind gardener, does good work.
And verdancy grows,
bud carefully opens
to a heavy crown on the end of its stem.
Fragrance that strengthens in evening's darkness
murmurs unfulfilled longing.
Comes the night.
A thrush plays its soft flute.
In the sky someone has raised a star.
One only.
The flower sighs.
Once only.

Puutarha, ihmisen tekemä.
Multa hoidettu monin käsin.
Elävä maa jota täytyy ruokkia.
Mato, sokea renki, tekee hyvää työtä.
Ja vehreys kasvaa,
nuppu varoen avautuu
raskaaksi kruunuksi varrelleen.
Tuoksu joka illan pimetessä voimistuu
humisee täyttymätöntä ikävää.
Tulee yö.
Rastas soittaa hiljaista huiluaan.
Taivaalle on joku nostanut tähden.
Yhden vain.
Kukka huokaa.
Kerran vain.

WHAT IS YOUR LIFE?

Dusk descends early in midday
and Youth comes like a dream
like a morning cloud
goes inside my skin
asks defiantly:
Who are you now? What are you?
Where are your big dreams
Is this as far as you've gone? What is your life?

For a little while we sit just the two of us,
drowsy, time falls asleep like a little girl.
I hold it in my hands for a moment, say:
it was born
under a free sky
into the wind, rain, and clouds.
It came like the grass, flower, bird,
like you came now.
It comes always, new.

INTO SNOWY NIGHT

Memories glide
clouds soft against the relentless sky
as though one were asleep and only dreaming.
I bring you close to me again
and your voice takes me to that coffee shop
where we sat as passengers.
And so the moment passed
into snowy night
where silence radiates from your skin.
I remain in the shade of that dream, alone,
in my eyes, images of you,
scent of a thousand lilies.

YOU LOOKED THE MONSTER IN THE EYE

You looked the monster in the eye,
nights passed by as torches burned,
nights, and days in a solid light,
every step ever further from oneself.

But, one more time, someone nameless
got you to turn back
in front of the last door,
you didn't even pull it open
that door, so invitingly ajar just a crack,
you turned around and with doll-like steps
walked to a more familiar train
to a smokey dream, aroma of tea and coal
hour by hour ever closer to light.

Yet you have been given additional time,
yet your bill with others is not totalled,
and the years' wheels squeak in a curve
when the train finally emerges from the tunnel
                          into the open.
You have come through it alive once again,
but your happiness has shrunk.
There are no longer many journeys to the land
                          of darkness,
not many chances to find your destiny,
when you yourself are soot black night.

TOMMY TABERMANN

TOMMY TABERMANN
(1947-   )

When Tommy Tabermann, at age 23, published his first collection of poems, *Ruusuja Rosa Luxemburgille* (Roses for Rosa Luxemburg, 1970), his style was immediately recognized as one of freshness, sensuality and sensitivity. A prolific and profoundly moving writer, Tabermann has published ten volumes of poetry and two novels in the last ten years. Recognized as a romantic, he is also very socially aware, and in his poems he makes no attempt to conceal his views in matters of social concern. But he is never dogmatic. He has undoubtedly been greatly influenced by the life of the industrial town of Karjaa where he lives.

In 1977 a selection of his poems from 1970-77 was published in a volume titled *Kukkiva kivi* (The Flowering Stone).

Tabermann has gained a wide readership because his poetry plumbs the depths of human experiences and transmits them into poems almost like song lyrics, fluctuating between irony and emotion, as in his book *Kipeästi keinuu keinumme* (Our Swing Sways Painfully, 1979). In a 1980 collection, *Intohimon panttivanki* (Hostage of Passion), he switches perspectives with astonishing agility, from the intimate to the objective and socially aware.

Tabermann was employed as a reporter for the Finnish Radio Broadcasting Corporation for ten years, 1969-1979.

SEAS ARE MY EYES, BIRCHES MY VOICE

Finland birthed me, the world suckled me.
Seas are my eyes, birches my voice,
the poor and suffering my sisters,
peace my beloved.
Long you waited for me, my cradle,
rock me once more,
rock me, rock me all the way to the womb.
My father's name is work, that is why
my toes are in the soil.
My mother's is tenderness, that is why
my head is in the stars.
Rock, my cradle, rock,
your son's tears are bright.
And in my home a fire in the stove
and on the wall Viipuri castle.
In the pot cabbage
and sometimes in the cupboard
half a bottle of liquor
Behind the flour sack once a mouse
but always on the bookshelf
a worker's pennant.
Behind the flour sack once a mouse
but always on the bookshelf a worker's pennant.
Rock, cradle, rock, your son's tears are bright
and soon he will go far away, far away.
Since Finland birthed me, the world
with blood and swallow's milk suckles me.

Sorretunrakkaus saapuu,
se lukitsee oven takanaan
ja asettuu sinuun iäksi
eikä petä koskaan.
Rakkaus saapuu,
se jättää matkalaukkunsa
ovenpieleen, pahimman varalta,
mutta riisuu vaatteensa.
Intohimo saapuu, se sytyttää ensin
sata kynttilää, tempaisee sitten
oven sdaranoiltaan ja
särkee ikkunat.
Jättää kaiken, kaiken tuulen varaan.

POSSESSIVE LOVE

Possessive love arrives,
it locks the door behind it
and settles in with you forever,
always predictable.
Love arrives,
it leaves its luggage
by the door, in case worse comes to worst,
but still undresses.
Passion arrives, first it lights
a hundred candles, then pulls
the door off its hinges and
breaks the windows.
Leaves everything, everything
                          to the care of the wind.

ARTO MELLERI

ARTO MELLERI
(1956-   )

The young poet Arto Melleri has published four volumes of poetry. His first collection, *Schlaageriseppele* (A Bouquet of Hit Tunes, 1978), was awarded the Kalevi Jäntti Memorial Prize. His writing has been said to represent the "new subjectivity" in Finnish poetry. It is exuberant and imaginative. He paints black utopias against which he contrasts his own emotions, from despair to fervent hope. He can also write lyrically and tenderly.

Melleri is an experimenter and has explored a variety of forms. He is active in radical youth theater. In 1978 he collaborated with two young playwrights to write *Pete Q.*, an avant-garde play that was a big hit. It established the point of view of the new theatrical generation.

Melleri's most recent poetry collections include: *Zoo* (1979), *Ilmalaiva "Italia"* (The Airship 'Italy,', 1980), and *Mau-Mau* (1982). In 1981 he edited an anthology of 26 young poets of the 1970s.

PROPORTIONS

A person's life: width of a hand
I have heard it said
I look at the early morning sky:
from star to star
even less
The happiness that you wait for, something that
cannot be measured, only possible
if not measured
At sunrise
small birds, without bursting,
sing out loud the morning dew,
the bright sound of countless droplets

LOVE'S ROCKY FOREST

No other road, no other way
to find each other:
groping, groping through insanity's mist,
the hospital's blue reflection in our faces
redeeming this feeling
torn petals,
in the fertile land of a common grave . . .
no other way: hinges of a gate
complain, a cloud
cuts across the moon's eye,
like a sword,
and from this dead perspective
a man's deeds revealed, horrible.
The whirlwind seizes
the Brontë sisters' silken petticoats
in love's stony forest,
the hunter's horn proclaims death,
hooves, silent
against the dry skin of moss
and shots echo,
gunpowder burns, the blood of a young goat congeals . . .

we grope toward each other,
the moon becomes translucent, the mist
boils on the ground
the forest ranger's dog howls
will we find each other, tonight?

WHAT IS THERE FOR US

Autumn is always a time
that is already gone: I sit under a rowan tree
    beside a shaky table
in a canvas chair that is faded from many rainy summers;
this is the only thing achievable,
the freedom not to hope.

I burn rubbish: yellowed account books
smoulder, price lists from the time of old money,
verification of one man's life work:
      went into debt, did not have time to pay it back,
bright flame reaches up to nothingness,
and the wind blows the smoke slantwise
toward the potato field, furrows.
The autumn sun turns the landscape into copper.

Not to hope, how difficult
    although, according to a song,
      the hole remains in the baker's hand,
what is there for us, after death,
we become poor soil.
The red-earthed storehouse doors
    are open: as though the white light of flour
were shining from the darkness, harvest is over,
and I am here, a baby cuckoo, born
with chaff ready in my throat.

Autumn is always a time
    that is already gone. Life: chaff dancing
        in a sieve.
The moon rises as though Hill's sauna
    were burning in a black field
white ashes . . . I no longer
guard it, something in me
has started to smoulder.

JUKKA VIENO

JUKKA VIENO
(1957-   )

In 1978, the year of the centenary of Eino Leino's birth, the esteemed literary prize of the Eino Leino Society went to the young poet Jukka Vieno for his first book, *Valkoisen liljan maa* (The Land of the White Lily, 1977). It was hailed in Finland as an especially promising literary debut. The originality of these poems owe much to Vieno's fearless use of the Finnish language. He works with sharp contrasts and explicit play on words. Many of his poems deal with a longing for death, despair with life, and the cruelty of love.

Vieno's second book, *Riippuvat puutarhat* (The Hanging Gardens, 1979), is a surrealist poem about disappointment in love.

OPEN YOUR FIST

Open your fist
and let your fingers fly.
There you have the whole universe.

Open your eyes
and look into them.
There are your opportunities.

Open your fist,
open your eyes,
open the door of the house of mourning
　　　　　　　　to let the tears flow.

WE MUST SHED OUR ILLUSIONS

Today,
August 6, the sun
may be
a new weapon of destruction.
Perhaps it won't set, will remain in place
until it falls
into the shade.
There we must dare to stay
and even more, dare
to be happy.
It grows
into night, and at night
I know
your body
is warm
and the sun doesn't
rise, set, we must shed
our illusions
or we will
lose them.

August 7
I open my arms:
the sun
climbs
into my lap.

LAND OF THE WHITE LILY

Once, winter stumbled into your bed,
a polar bear fell asleep, paw on your neck,
growled in its sleep about the Land of the White Lily.
You saw white everywhere,
found no lily under the snow.

That is how you got your gloomy nature,
grief that plows a field of sorrow on your forehead,
words that speak ill of you,
black tears that sprout for their own pleasure
when you plant them in the furrows.

Chilled, you raged as the Grim Reaper,
flattened, you no longer had a head
when you turned to see who hit you,
the field fell asleep, murmurs flew away.

ACKNOWLEDGMENTS

ANHAVA, HELENA
"My Sons Have Grown to Manhood," "Among the Grieving One Should Speak Softly," and "Childhood Summers," all from *Murheellisen Kuullen on Puhuttava Hiljaa*, 1972.

ANHAVA, TUOMAS
"The Sky Has Wings," from *Uuden Runon Kauneimmat I*, 1970; "May 1964 V" and "I Sleep to the Patter of the Rain," both from *Runojen Kirja*, 1977.

HAAVIKKO, PAAVO
"When I Now Tell You About the Emperor" and "Recorders of Life," both from *Runojen Kirja*, 1977; "I Look Outside," from *Runoni rakkaudesta*, 1981.

HELLAAKOSKI, AARO
"Moonlight in the Forest," from *Jääpeili*, 1928; "Hawk," from *Elegiasta oodiin*, 1921.

JYLHÄ YRJÖ
"Holy Night" and "A Meeting in the Forest," both in *Kiirastuli*, 1941; "Enemmän," from *Runoni rakkaudesta*, 1981.

KAILAS, UUNO
"In This Small Country," "My Son," and "Guilty Man," all from *Runojen Kirja*, 1977; "The House," from *Uni ja Kuolema*, 1931.

KAJAVA, VILJO
"I Am a Guitar," from *Runojen kirja*, 1977; "Father is Leaving," *Valitut Runot*, 1969; "Songs of Sorrow, Spring 1918," from *Kiila 30*, 1966; "When I was very little. . . ," and "The sky went before me. . . ," both from *Valitut Runot*, 1969; "Love Is Not Cleansed by Fire," from *Runojen kirja, 1977*.

KILPI, EEVA
"He Stepped Inside My Door" and "And Dreams Paled," both from Laulu rakkaudesta, 1972; "Even Nature Gives You No Choice . . ." and "What Is This Sound. . . ," both from Terveisin, 1976; "The Fifth Day" and "Where Behind the Night Did You Get Lost," from Ennen Kuolemaa, 1982; "One Morning the Earth Stirred," from Laulu rakkaudesta, 1972; "Weather Fore-casters" and "Thistle," from Terveisin, 1976; "A Midsummer's Rose," from Terveisin, 1976; "Tomorrow I Will Heat the Sauna," from Laulu Rakkaudesta, 1972.

KIRSTINÄ VÄINÖ
"You Will See Far," from *Suomen lyriikkaa tänään*, 1969; "This Rocky Land," "Propaganda Art," and "Fierce Old Trees," from *Talo Maalla*, 1969.

LEINO, EINO
"Äijö's Song," from *Helkavirsiä II*, 1916; "I," from *Halla*, 1908; "Drifter's Song," from *Shemeikan murhe*, 1924; "Nocturne," from *Talvi-yö*, 1905; "Goodness," from *Shemeikan murhe*, 1924.

233

MANNER, EEVA-LIISA

"Here," from *Tämä matka*, 1956; "Into the Silence of the Forest," "Assimilation," "A Walk," and "Speculation," all from *Kirjoitettu kivi*, 1966; "Bach," from *Tämä matka*, 1956; "Last Year in Capricorn," from *Kirjoitettu kivi*, 1966; "From My Life I Make a Poem," from *Tämä matka*, 1956.

MELLERI, ARTO

"Proportions," "What Is There For Us," and "Love's Rocky Forest," all from *Ilmalaiva 'Italia,'* 1980

MERI, VEIJO

"Rhythm," from *Toinen sydän*, 1978; "The World is Round," from *Mielen lähtälaskenta*, 1976; "Bucharest" and "When I Was Young," both from *Toinen sydän*, 1978.

MERILUOTO, AILA

"The Stone God," from *Lasimaalaus*, 1946; "In the Year 4 After Father, from *Varokaa putoilevia enkeleitä*, 1977; "On the Shore," from *Asumattomiin*, 1963; "I Look at Your Land," from *Varokaa putolevia enkeleitä*, 1977.

MUSTAPÄÄ, P.

"A Memory," from *Runoni rakkaudesta*, 1981; "Folk Melody" and "A Song," both from *P. Mustapään runoja*, 1967; "Lachesis Net," from *Runon Vuosikymmenet 1897-1947*, 1967.

MÄKELÄ, HANNU

"Garden," from *Illan varjo*, 1979; "What Is Your Life," from *Ikään kuin ihminen*, 1980; "Into Snowy Night," from *Illan varjo*, 1979; "You Looked the Monster in the Eye," from *Ikään kuin ihminen*, 1980.

NIEMINEN, PERTTI

"That's Not a Tiger," from *Suomen lyriikkää*, 1969; "My Sister," from *Huomisella vielä omat huolensa*, 1979; "I Drink the Wine of Your Dreams," from *Uuden runon kauneimmat I*, 1970; "When I Neared Fifty" and "They Were Pure Gold," both from *Huomisella vielä omat huolensa*, 1979.

REKOLA, MIRKKA

"Among Dark Trees," from *Kuutamourkka*, 1981; "In This Wind" and "You Remember the Elk," from *Uuden runon kauneimmat I*, 1970.

SAARIKOSKI, PENTTI

"A Long Journey," from *Kuljen missä kuljen*, 1966; "I Live in Helsinki," "Parliament Had Been Dissolved," "A Good Society," "The Sun Sets, Sun Rises," and "History of the Revolution," all from *Tähänastiset runot*, 1978; "XIII," from *Tanssilattia vuorella*, 1977; "XXX," from *Tanssiinkutsu*, 1980.

SAARITSA, PENTTI

"Salt of Pleasure," "We Were Suntanned Gods," and "Voice of My Brothers," all from *Nautinnon suola*, 1978.

TABERMANN, TOMMY

"Seas Are My Eyes, Birches My Voice," from *Kukkiva kivi, Valitut runot 1970-1977*, 1978; "Possessive Love," from *Runoni rakkaudesta*, 1981.

TURKKA, SIRKKA

"Poems of Pain," "I See Trees Falling," Thus the Trees Change Places," "Tenderness Closed Like a Flower," "When the Sovereign Asks," "You Are Born Again and Again," all from *Kaunis hallitsija*, 1981.

TURTIAINEN, ARVO

"Shoemaker Nikke," from *Runojen kirja*, 1977; "Loveliest Poem," from *Runoni rakkaudesta*, 1981; "Ballad of Herman's Rose (Parts: Helsinki, I, III, and V)," from *Runoja 1934-1968*, 1976.

VALA, KATRI

"String of Pearls," from *Runoni rakkaudesta*, 1981; "The Child Plays," from *Kootut runot*, 1948; "The Bridge," from *Paluu*, 1934; "Winter Has Come," from *Pesäpuu palaa*, 1942.

VAMMELVUO, ANJA

"Small Boys," from *Uuden runon kauneimmat I*, 1970; "Aleksandra Kollontay," from *Kiila 30*, 1966; "Another Spring, Another Year" and "Even the Mirror Dies," both from *Totuuden iskut*, 1973.

VIENO, JUKKA

"Open Your Fist," "We Must Shed Our Illusions," and "Land of the White Lily," all from *Valkoisen liljan maa*, 1977.

SELECTED BIBLIOGRAPHY

Books

Ahokas, Jaakko. *A History of Finnish Literature.* Indiana University, Bloomington, Indiana, 1973.

Dauenhauer, Richard and Philip Binham, Editors, *Snow in May,* An Anthology of Finnish Writing 1945-1972. Fairleigh Dickinson University Press, Rutherford, New Jersey, 1978.

Eskola, Antti and Katarina Eskola, Editors. *Kirjallisuus Suomessa* (Literature in Finland). Kustannusosakeyhtiö Tammi, Helsinki, 1974.

Haavikko, Ritva, Editor. *Kirjailijat puhuvat — Tulenkantajat* (Writers Speak — Torch Bearers). Suomalaisen Kirjallisuuden Seura, Helsinki, 1976.

Kolehmainen, John I. *Epic of the North,* The Story of Finland's Kalevala. The Northwestern Publishing Company, New York Mills, Minnesota, 1973.

Laitinen, Kai. *Suomen kirjallisuus 1917-1967* (Finland's Literature 1917-1967). Otava, Helsinki, 1967.

_____ *Suomen kirjallisuuden historia* (The History of Finnish Literature). Otava, Helsinki, 1981.

Laitinen, Kai, Juhani Niemi and Igmar Svedberg. *Finlands litteratur efter år 1965.* Edited by Marja-Leena Rautalin, Suomen kirjastoseura-Finlands biblioteksförening, Helsingfors, 1975.

Leino, Eino. *Whitsongs* (Helkavirsiä I, 1903). Translated from the Finnish by Keith Bosley, Introduction by Michael Branch, The Menard Press, London, 1978.

Linnilä, Kai, Editor. *Kiila 30* (The Wedge 30). Tammi, Helsinki, 1966.

Lomas, Herbert, Translator. *Territorial Song,* New Writing in Finland. London Magazine Editions, London, 1981.

Lönnrot, Elias, Compiled by. *The Kalevala,* or Poems of the Kaleva District. Translated by Francis Peabody Magoun, Jr., Harvard University Press, Cambridge, Massachusetts, 1963.

Ravila, Paavo. *Finnish Literary Reader.* Indiana University, Bloomington, Indiana, 1965.

Saarenheimo, Kerttu. *Tulenkantajat* (Torch Bearers). Werner Söderström Osakeyhtiö, Helsinki, 1966.

Tarkka, Pekka. *Suomalaisia nykykirjailijoita* (Contemporary Finnish Writers). Tammi, Helsinki, 1980.

Periodicals

Books from Finland. Editor-in-Chief, Kai Laitinen. A literary quarterly published in Helsinki, Finland. Issues from 1976 until the present.

Poetry East. Editors, Richard Jones and Kate Daniels. An international magazine of poetry, translations, criticism, interviews, and art. Number six, Fall 1981 issue contains a special section on Finnish poetry. Published in Earlysville, Virginia.

Scandinavian Review. A quarterly publication of the American-Scandinavian Foundation, New York. Finnish poetry in English translation is published in issues 1/79 (Paavo Haavikko), 2/80 (Tuomas Anhava), 4/80 (Pentti Saarikoski), and 2/82 (Tabermann and others). Issue 4/82 contains an article, "The Postmodern Poetry and Poetics of Pentti Saarikoski," by Vincent B. Leitch.

World Literature Today. Editor, Ivar Ivask. A Literary Quarterly of the University of Oklahoma. Winter 1980 is a special issue on Finnish literature.

TRANSLATOR

AILI JARVENPA is a second generation Finnish American whose parents immigrated to Minnesota from Finland before World War I. She is a graduate of the University of Minnesota and a retired Minneapolis high school teacher. North Star Press has published two books of her poetry, *Half Immersed* (1978) and *Tuohela* (1982). Her poems have also appeared in various literary journals and anthologies, including *Storystone, Lake Street Review, Sing Heavenly Muse!, North Country Anvil, Full Circle II,* and *Finnish Americana.* In 1981 her translations of poems by Eeva Kilpi were published in the poetry journal, *Milkweed Chronicle.* She has also translated the "voice over" for the Finnish American film, *Tradition Bearers,* and the filmed reaction in Finland to the showing there of the nationally award-winning documentary film, *Finnish American Lives,* both films produced by Dr. Michael Loukinen. She has translations forthcoming in a 1983 issue of *Finnish Americana* and in a collection of Finnish folk tales to be published in English translation by the Finnish American Literary Heritage Foundation of Portland, Oregon.

PHOTOGRAPHERS

OLIVER JARVENPA is a graduate of the University of Minnesota and a retired wildlife biologist whose articles and photography have appeared in professional publications, including the *Journal of the Minnesota Academy of Science* and the *Minnesota Conservation Volunteer.* For a number of years he headed the Ecological Services Section of the Minnesota Department of Natural Resources. His photographs in this volume were taken in Finland in 1978. A second generation Finnish American, he is married to Aili Jarvenpa.

ROBERT JARVENPA is an Associate Professor of Anthropology at the State University of New York at Albany. His articles on ecological adaptations, social and economic change, and inter-ethnic relations among the Chipewyan and Cree Indians in northern Canada have appeared, together with his photography, in numerous publications. He was a Visiting Fulbright Professor at the University of Helsinki in 1979. During that year his photographs in this volume were taken. He is currently initiating field research on agrarian ecology and decision making in Finland and is the recipient of a grant from the Finnish Ministry of Education. He is the son of Aili and Oliver Jarvenpa.

INTRODUCER

K. BÖRJE VÄHÄMÄKI was born in Vaasa, Finland. He received his Licentiate of Philosophy degree from Åbo Akademi, Turku, Finland, in 1975 and came to Minnesota the same year. He is currently Associate Professor of Finnish Language and Literature at the University of Minnesota. Professor Vähämäki has held appointments at the University of Oulu and Åbo Akademi. Interested in linguistics as well as literature, he has published articles in both fields. He has authored a book, *Existence and Identity—A Study of the Semantics and Syntax of Existential Sentences in Finnish*, now in press, and is a co-translator of *Finnish Short Stories*, 1982. He is a contributor to the review section of the journal, *World Literature Today*.

239

NEW RIVERS ABROAD

Harry Brander, ELVES DON'T GET CANCER (poems), translated from the Dutch by Judith Schavrian, with drawings by John Dobbs, $3.00

Siv Cedering (Fox), translator, TWO SWEDISH POETS: FRIBERG & PALM, $2.00

Lars Gustafsson, SELECTED POEMS, translated from the Swedish by Robin Fulton, with photographs by Arthur Tress, $2.50 (paper), $5.00 (cloth)

Jerzy Harasymowicz, PLANTING BEECHES (poems), translated from the Polish by Victor Contoski, $2.00

Aili Jarvenpa, editor and translator, SALT OF PLEASURE: TWENTIETH-CENTURY FINNISH POETRY, with an introduction by K. Börje Vähämäki and photographs by Oliver and Robert Jarvenpa, $7.50

Nicholas Kolumban, editor and translator, TURMOIL IN HUNGARY: AN ANTHOLOGY OF TWENTIETH-CENTURY HUNGARIAN POETRY, $6.00

Miodrag Pavlovich, THE CONQUEROR IN CONSTANTINOPLE (poems), translated from the Serbo-Croatian by Joachim Neugroschel, $2.00

David Rosenthal, editor and translator, MODERN CATALAN POETRY, with artwork by Picasso, Miro, and other Catalan artists, $6.00

Tadeusz Rozewicz, UNEASE (poems), translated from the Polish by Victor Contoski, with woodcuts by Gaylord Schanilec, $4.50

Brian Swann and Ruth Feldman, editors, ITALIAN POETRY TODAY, with artwork from contemporary Italian artists and an introduction by Glauco Cambon, $7.95

Derick Thomson, THE FAR ROAD, translated from the Gaelic by the author, $2.00 (paper), $4.50 (cloth)

Tristan Tzara, PRIMELE POEME/FIRST POEMS, translated from the Rumanian by Michael Impey and Brian Swann, $4.00 (paper) $10.00 (cloth)